Praise for *Toward a Secret Sky*

"This is a marvelous book on the outer and inner meaning of pilgrimage. Fearless and disarmingly honest, it's simultaneously a pilgrimage into the heart-mind of a spiritual warrior. Kim Roberts distills a lifetime of gritty experience into an offering that is sure to illuminate your own journey. Wisdom and kindness shine through every page, and practical advice leaves you well-equipped to set out on your own path of discovery. These are footsteps worth following."
—**Andrew Holecek**, author, *Dream Yoga*

"In a world full of promises for spiritual growth, how does one recognize an authentic path or teacher? Where does one even begin? Roberts responds to this very question by providing a compassionate 'road map' full of personal anecdotes, traditional wisdom, and practical advice necessary for navigating the terrain of one's own spiritual adventure! A kind and accessible book that supports the human longing for a meaningful life."
—**Elizabeth Mattis Namgyel**, author, *The Logic of Faith*

"With simple and profound practices, Kim Roberts guides us to explore our inner landscape in the context of the external world and *Toward a Secret Sky* magnificently illuminates the path of the most sacred journey we will ever take. This beautiful book is a compass that I will return to again and again."
—**Nancy Levin**, author, *Jump . . . and Your Life Will Appear*

"Finally a modern book about the practice of pilgrimage, with touching personal stories, historical research, and exercises for the reader to explore. Even if you never make an outer pilgrimage, this book is a fascinating guide, and if you are contemplating one, an essential companion."
—**Lama Tsultrim Allione**, author, *Wisdom Rising*

"A marvelous guide to the path of the pil
Kim Roberts knows whereof she speak
—**Sean N**

D1316440

"In the Buddhist literatures of India and Tibet, one reads of the awakening of inclinations established by meaningful and fortunate encounters in previous lifetimes and also of the awakening of an interior lineage that one had neither noticed nor suspected. Perhaps one had no hope of it. Perhaps one wishes it would go back to sleep. Good news or bad, once awake, it will not leave one alone. What to do? Having herself followed insistent, inconvenient, if also uplifting, intimations of unknown lands, both inside and outside, Kim Roberts has written lucidly and with the knowledge of a seasoned explorer of the steps one may take toward a destination somewhere beyond the horizon but also perhaps close to home, if only one knew the direction in which to head out, the quicksand to avoid, and the tricks of charlatans who will take what one has and leave one with nothing other than a sense of trespass. She's given us a map for troubled times. Let us welcome its arrival and consider her counsel carefully."

—Jules B. Levinson, translator, *Essential Practice*
by Khenchen Thrangu Rinpoche

"I love this book! It is a user-friendly guidebook for all spiritual practitioners, regardless of the specific path chosen. Kim Roberts expresses the wisdom of her own years of deep practice, inner exploration, and training. As an experienced yoga teacher, counselor, writer, and mentor, she shares the ins and outs of spiritual practice that shine with compassion and humor. Her stories make the journey come alive with such grace. You can't help but want to dig in, keep reading, AND put everything into your own life."

—Kate H. Feldman, MSW, LCSW, founding member,
Kripalu Center for Yoga & Health, cofounder of
The Conscious Relationships Institute

"We thoroughly love and support the idea of pilgrimage. Whether it's the inner journey inspired by life, yoga, poetry, meditation, or travel afar, we're all in!"

—Ganga White, author, *Yoga Beyond Belief*
and **Tracey Rich**, director, White Lotus Foundation

"*Toward a Secret Sky* is engaging, personal, and deep. Kim Roberts brings her honesty and humor to the question of pilgrimage: how might we step into the unknown with the intention of making awareness and kindness the life-giving center of our lives. This book is both practical and inspiring. If you're ready to invite more openness and disturbance into your experiencing, read it."

—Bruce Tift, author, *Already Free*

TOWARD
A
SECRET SKY

TOWARD A SECRET SKY

Creating Your Own Modern Pilgrimage

KIM ROBERTS

ixia
PRESS

Mineola, New York

Bibliographical Note

Toward a Secret Sky: Creating Your Own Modern Pilgrimage is a new work, first published by Ixia Press in 2019.
This guidebook is not intended as a substitute for studying with a qualified teacher or guru. The author assumes that if you are reading this book you already have developed a relationship to yoga or meditation. She offers examples of how pilgrimage might look so that you will be inspired to embark on your own spiritual journey. Her hope is you will develop the confidence in your own wisdom to guide your steps along the path.

Library of Congress Cataloging-in-Publication Data

Names: Roberts, Kim, 1965– author.
Title: Toward a secret sky : creating your own modern pilgrimage / Kim Roberts.
Description: Mineola, New York : Ixia Press, [2019]
Identifiers: LCCN 2019000878| ISBN 9780486832272 | ISBN 0486832279
Subjects: LCSH: Pilgrims and pilgrimages. | Women—Religious life.
Classification: LCC BL619.P5 R55 2019 | DDC 203/.51—dc23
LC record available at https://lccn.loc.gov/2019000878

Ixia Press
An imprint of Dover Publications, Inc.

Manufactured in the United States by LSC Communications
83227901   2019
www.doverpublications.com/ixiapress

This is love: to fly toward a secret sky,
to cause a hundred veils to fall each moment.
First to let go of life.
Finally, to take a step without feet;
to regard this world as invisible,
and to disregard what appears to be the self.

—Mewlana Jalaluddin Rumi

Contents

Foreword

This is the story of a practitioner who traveled to many parts of Asia on a journey that resulted in her becoming a teacher of yoga. In this book she describes the path that took her eventually to the teachings and practice of the Vajrayana. This book may be of interest to those who wish to read about how yoga and higher meditation can be combined. Kimberly Roberts, on her path of discovery, became my student.

—Khenchen Thrangu Rinpoche
Sarnath, India
March 2019

What an incredible relief it is to understand
that the ultimate pilgrimage
is right in the center of our own hearts.

—Richard Freeman

TOWARD A SECRET SKY

Part 1

The Call

The Call

You hear the call in your own unique manner. It arrives as a whisper or a yelp, a gentle nudge or an agonizing cry. However it arrives, you hear it loud and clear, and you know. It's time.

Time for what? Ah, that, you may have no idea. You feel the urge, the momentum of something guiding you somewhere, but you may have no idea where. But what is unmistakable is that it's time for a Change. Something inside—the inner guide, no doubt—knows you are ready to evolve and provides appropriate circumstances to help nudge or shove you in the right direction. Sometimes these circumstances are merely uncomfortable as you lean in to your fears. Often they are disastrous and excruciating as your whole world falls apart.

Either you listen, or you don't. If you listen, you are about to embark on a pilgrimage.

So you move in a direction that has some reference point—a stated destination, an outcome, a geography. You have to start somewhere. Some idea has been born that generates enough interest to get up and walk, fly, ride, or drive to a specific place. Or perhaps the destination is not yet known and you have to keep adjusting the path according to a set of criteria. You might not really know where you're going. You get inklings, signs, messages, auspicious coincidences. You feel your way forward.

You are moving "toward"; it is definitely not "to." You are not going "to" somewhere, because if you knew exactly where you were going it would cancel out the mysterious nature of the journey. A pilgrimage is an unknown destination—even if the geographical locale you set out to travel to might be somewhere on the map. The whole idea of pilgrimage implies an element of mystery and divine intervention. You learn to face unforeseen challenges and adapt to a new set of circumstances that mirrors the process of transforming the mind. You learn to rest in not knowing. When you accept the mission of a pilgrimage, in essence, you sign up for these obstacles. After all, you want change. You want growth—or at least to widen your horizons—otherwise you wouldn't embark on a pilgrimage in the first place.

And yet your circumstances might not allow you to wander to the farthest reaches of the planet, or even take a week off. No problem. Your pilgrimage may be of the most subtle sort: that of transforming your view through an inner journey alone. What's most important when answering the call is an attitude of openness, a willingness to venture into new, uncharted territory. That territory is the mind.

1

Start Where You Are

How to Embark on Pilgrimage

How do you go about taking that leap for yourself? What if you don't even know what leap to take?

My intention is to help you start exploring the possibility of going on a spiritual journey, whether or not you leave home. Since my background is drenched in Eastern spiritual practices— Ashtanga yoga and Buddhist meditation from a Tibetan lineage— most of what I share comes from those traditions. My journey has mostly been through South and Southeast Asia. My hope is to offer guidance for how to negotiate the path of yoga and meditation as a lifelong practice of transformation.

When you hear the call, you notice that you suddenly want to do something new and different or even slightly outrageous. What seems safe and known starts to lose its appeal. Your material belongings may start to feel more like a burden, and you may question your reference points.

You might start off by learning a practice at your local community center or yoga studio. If you already practice yoga or meditation, perhaps you go deeper by doing a short retreat. Maybe you're ready to do something outside of your comfort zone.

I'll guide you to find answers to these questions:

- ❧ How do I start? (chapter 3)
- ❧ Where should I go? (chapter 4)
- ❧ What would my pilgrimage look like? (chapters 7, 11, 14, and 15)

I've also created a whole section of resources[1] to get you started and keep you on track:

- ❧ How to develop a meditation practice
- ❧ Where to do a retreat
- ❧ What to read

Pilgrimage indicates a journey, and this book outlines not only how to prepare for, organize, and embark on such a journey, but also shares highlights from my various pilgrimages over the years throughout South and Southeast Asia. In these pages I share the things I never had the time to delve into while teaching a yoga class, as well as the personal stories that were not appropriate to share with my therapy clients. Meditators will learn how simple yoga techniques can benefit their sitting practice. Yoga practitioners will expand and deepen their understanding of asana. Practitioners of yoga and meditation will gain insights into bringing their practice into the world to be of benefit to our ailing planet and its inhabitants. Writing practices at the ends of chapters will let you experience the power of journaling.

This book is a culmination of over twenty-six years of experience I've earned through meeting with my teachers, long daily practices, intensive study, and living with reptiles in bug-infested huts, taking cold-water bucket-baths. Part of the journey is confronting yourself and your attachment to comfort. It's also about turning every day into a pilgrimage, and that requires a shift in attitude.

Think of this as your guidebook, your journal, and your workbook. I'll be your invisible guide and friend as you make your own pilgrimage.

Not sure where to start? I'll show you.

What Is Pilgrimage?

A pilgrimage is always at least two things—a literal journey and a spiritual journey. Though it involves a geographical moving about, it also requires a psychological shift of the deepest sort.

Pilgrimage can mean a day trip to a holy shrine, or it can denote a series of adventures lasting decades. It is above all a psycho-spiritual journey, usually to a place of religious significance or to meet a master of wisdom, with elements of both an inner and outer journey. Primarily, I think what characterizes a pilgrimage is that we are forced to face our fears head-on.

The *Oxford Dictionary* defines pilgrimage as:

1.1 A journey to a place of particular interest or significance.

1.2 literary Life viewed as a journey.

Merriam-Webster's Collegiate Dictionary (11th Edition) defines it as:

1 : a journey of a pilgrim; *especially*: one to a shrine or a sacred place

2 : the course of life on earth

Travel—especially in a foreign country—forces you to come to terms with aspects of yourself you might not confront in your everyday life. Things come up when your environment is unknown, unexpected, changing, and often challenging.

So you might pack up your home, put your life on hold, and set off traveling through Asia with an open stretch of time ahead of you. You hope to take stock, and discover a new angle on life. Maybe make a transition in your career.

What starts out as a journey to find peace, however, can end up being anything but peaceful. Often when we are confronted with things that challenge our outlook of the world, we struggle to maintain our sense of identity. If you are operating on old beliefs that no longer serve you, that might be a good thing. This is precisely the value of a pilgrimage: it shatters your identity, so that you can reintegrate around a more up-to-date, authentic version of who you are.

While I've done my fair share of day-tripping to shrines and treks to sacred sites, I find Oxford's second definition most provocative—life viewed as a journey. This is what captures my curiosity as I grow older: How do I live my life as a journey?

But a pilgrimage is more than just a journey. When you set out on an adventure with the right intention, you set in motion a process that can transform your life. This is the point of pilgrimage: transformation.

When you take the first step on a pilgrimage, you put your life in the hands of a higher wisdom. You accept that you cannot control outcomes, and surrender to the process of becoming who you truly are. You accept that there is some divine purpose to your life even if it is as simple as tending your own garden. It may not be as grandiose as the plans you had laid out for yourself, but it is your unique gift to offer the world. There is a huge amount of trust involved that requires a willingness to be with whatever arises along the path.

Pilgrimage is about learning to adapt to new situations. It's about opening your mind to new possibilities. You have to release expectations of how you thought your journey would unfold and let the path reveal itself regardless of your preferences. You learn to be flexible in the face of sudden change or conflict.

When you can appreciate the ups and downs with equanimity, then traveling—whether or not you leave your home territory—becomes a joyful practice of observation. Rather than judging unfamiliar traditions, you start to see there are other ways of doing things. From eating, daily rituals, relating to death, family and intimacy—all cultures treat these in their own way. You can start to question if the way you learned to do things works for you. It gives you options to make changes or adjustments to your own life if you choose to.

When I spent a year in India—which, by the way, is one of the best places to travel to confront yourself—I realized that my American culture had ingrained in me certain values that I took to be truths. For example, my culture proposes that material wealth is a way to achieve happiness. When I lived among Indians, I saw a different way of looking at things that completely changed how I perceive and approach my life. The experience radically shifted my perspective. When I made my yoga practice a higher priority than pursuing a professional career, it was the first time in my life I'd actually relaxed fully.

Another value among rural Indians is that it's completely normal to brush your teeth by the side of the road. I'm not sure I'll ever adopt this practice, but it did open my mind to new possibilities.

You know how to make God laugh, right? Make plans. Pilgrimage might be about making friends with the fact that things don't go as planned.

You journey to meet a teacher, then discover he is at the place you just left. You take precautions against respiratory illness, only to get stomach flu. Or you sign up for a private interview with a guru on the day he has fallen ill. You reserve a guesthouse months ahead of time, only to show up and have no room. Then you can't sleep all night because of the loud music of neighborhood festivities, only to get the e-mail the next morning that you were invited to the party.

Faced with these events, you have choices. You could sulk, pout and yell, wallowing in poverty mentality. Or you can throw up your hands (as well as the corners of your mouth) and take a deep breath.

Resistance is futile. In fact it makes it worse. Pilgrimage is above all an opportunity to see our expectations for what they are—illusions created by a conceptual mind that we then grasp at—and to let go.

Primarily, I think what characterizes a pilgrimage is that we are forced to face our fears head-on. The whole point is to expose ego's sneaky ways to a higher wisdom in order for transformation to occur.

But pilgrimage is not for the faint of heart. It requires a certain amount of stamina and strength. The best-made plans fall to bits, and things rarely go as expected. There is wisdom in learning to let go of your agenda. You learn to tolerate the tension of ego straining against its imagined edges. So if you are up for a wild ride, and an opportunity to push your limits, then join me for an adventure.

The big question I invite you to contemplate along the journey is this:

How can you live your life as a pilgrimage or sacred journey?

What is it that characterizes a pilgrimage and how can you re-create that in your life to forge an authentic spiritual path? The story of a Buddhist saint called Naropa seems relevant here.

Ancient Pilgrimage

Naropa was an Indian prince who lived in the eleventh century. He was also a scholar and respected professor at Nalanda University, near Bodhgaya. This is where the Buddha was sitting under the Bodhi tree when he attained enlightenment.

One day as Naropa was studying the Buddhist texts, a crone appeared to him in a vision and asked if he understood what he was reading. He answered, "yes," and the woman seemed pleased.

Then she asked if he understood the real meaning of what he

was reading. Again he answered yes (he probably added an Indian head wobble), and she threw a fit. It turned out the crone was the deity Vajrayogini in disguise. She appeared in all her wrath and fury and chastised him for his reply. He didn't understand the inner meaning at all.

He got the message: He didn't have any experience to go along with his book learning.

So Naropa decided to quit his prestigious position at the university to search for a guru. He needed someone who could teach him the inner meaning to gain this experience. He asked around and heard that a great and realized teacher called Tilopa could give him these teachings.

Tilopa was an Indian king who had attained full enlightenment through his own diligent meditation practice. He is recognized as the founding father of one of the four major schools of Tibetan Buddhism, the Kagyu lineage. After weeks of traveling through the mountains—we would imagine cold, tired, and hungry—Naropa finally found Tilopa by the side of a river. Naropa asked him to be his teacher, but Tilopa said no and ran away from him.

Naropa was distraught. He followed him for months—eventually years—through harsh landscapes, but over and over, Tilopa kept running away. Naropa was beside himself with disappointment.

Finally, Naropa caught up with Tilopa, who was sitting on a high cliff. Again he asked Tilopa to be his teacher.

Tilopa responded, "If you were really desperate and determined to learn about the teachings, you would obey my order to jump off this cliff without any hesitation because you would understand how important it is to follow the commands of your master."

Naropa jumped. He broke every bone in his body. Tilopa flew down to Naropa and asked, "Did that hurt?"

Naropa said yes.

Tilopa gently touched Naropa's body and he was instantly healed.

Tilopa tested Naropa again and again like this, causing him pain, humiliation, and sorrow. But he would not give him the teachings Naropa desired.

After twelve years of this, Naropa was destitute—he was getting suicidal. Naropa pleaded with Tilopa to give him the profound teachings.

Tilopa bellowed at him, "You are not yet pure enough to be introduced to the nature of mind!" In a fit of fury, Tilopa removed his shoe and slapped Naropa's face so hard that Naropa fainted.

When he regained consciousness, Naropa had attained a state of realization.

Tilopa then explained to him, "The fact that I led you into so many painful circumstances does not mean that I am a cruel person. Your negative karma could not be purified by your own effort alone. Only by experiencing hardship could you purify the negative karma that prevented you from realizing the ultimate nature of Buddhahood."

So after twelve long years, Naropa succeeded in receiving the teachings—and more importantly the experience—he had set out to find.

Modern Pilgrimage

Things are a bit easier these days for those who want to receive teachings.

It no longer requires an arduous voyage to remote locations across the globe—you can book a discount flight on Air Asia to an obscure region of India and be there within a matter of days or even hours. You can go online and register for a three-month retreat in the Himalayas, or download ancient texts and have secret, esoteric teachings at your fingertips. What used to involve pain and hardship is now a matter of convenience and exotic whim.

With the advent of the Internet, the whole nature of pilgrimage has changed forever. Go to Amazon—dot com, not the river—and you can purchase tantric texts on the nature of mind, translated into English, with commentaries by realized masters. You can now Google Krishnamacharya and download, for free, his seminal text on Ashtanga Yoga (Yoga Makaranda) that essentially brought yoga to the masses in the West. Before Google, you had to first somehow hear about this great teacher, find out where he was, go there, and convince him to give these teachings to you. Total time required? Probably your entire life and all your savings. These days, the whole thing could be accomplished in three minutes.

But would you get the same understanding? The benefits of pilgrimage have not been replaced by the convenience of receiving teachings. Ironically, you might even underestimate the depth of these wisdom traditions because of their accessibility. My sense is that one earns the "wisdom" of the ancient teachings through learning how to manage adversity. You can't buy wisdom, or store it on your hard drive.

A two hundred-hour teacher training program at a luxury resort in the tropics is a much different experience than an eight-month trek across a dust-blown Tibetan plateau to find a teacher who may or may not still be alive or willing to share the wisdom you seek.

You and I have access to wisdom teachings that would have taken seekers a lifetime to acquire just a couple of decades ago. And yet we lose the adventure in this scenario—the hardship and uncertainty that were inevitably part of the pilgrimage. So does it still count?

We might be tempted to treat these sacred teachings as if they were our just due. I wonder if we appreciate them in the same way we would have if we had been forced to leave our homes and risk life and limb to get them.

But this is our situation. We can't go back in time. So if we are to benefit from having quick and easy access to secret mystical teachings, then perhaps we need to reevaluate what we do with them—how we put them into practice.

With yoga studios popping up like fast-food restaurants around the world , more and more people have access to—or have at least heard of—yoga and meditation. Consumer mentality turns these sacred tools into commodities, often watering down the wisdom most seekers receive.

Given the modern context, where spiritual teachers now come to give teachings in concert halls of major Western cities, and livestream tantric teachings, must we expand our understanding of pilgrimage? How do we undertake a true pilgrimage given these modern conveniences?

It's up to us to preserve the power of the teachings by putting them into practice. We do this through continuous inquiry, on the meditation cushion, and on the yoga mat.

A New Paradigm

As yoga's popularity has boomed in mainstream culture, many traditionalists wonder if the integrity of the teachings has been compromised. But I have a different take—I think anyplace you start is valid. The beauty of yoga—especially a self-directed practice like Ashtanga Vinyasa yoga—is that it is an easy entry into a spiritual path. It's an excellent starting-off point for a pilgrimage.

Taking guided classes at a yoga studio is great at the beginning of your journey, in order to learn the technique and parameters of a practice. But when you do your own yoga, you are forced to confront yourself in a way that can easily be avoided in a class setting. This is imperative if you are to proceed along the path of awakening. So at a certain point, I feel it is important to develop your own self-guided routine, rather than relying on structured classes at a yoga studio.

Without some self-direction and awareness of the path, a yoga student may simply adopt a blind faith type of allegiance to the practice and only work on perfecting postures. To avoid this, some awareness of the larger journey—and the meaning of that journey—is important. Otherwise, yoga, or any spiritual discipline, can become just another way to check out of daily reality into a fantasy zone of magical hopes and, if there are positive results to show for one's efforts, self-aggrandizement. This is called spiritual bypassing—I'll get into that in chapter 8.

Another pitfall is what Chögyam Trungpa Rinpoche called spiritual materialism—appropriating spiritual practice for ego's benefit. Spiritual materialism is so rampant that it's difficult to present an alternative. You engage in spiritual materialism every time you go to yoga class expecting it to make you feel better— any time you expect some type of benefit from your expenditure. Spiritual development is not a transactional relationship—results are not dependent on how much you pay. Logic says that if I spend this much time and effort on something I'll have a proportionate reward. Spirituality is not logical.

It is not uncommon for practitioners of yoga or meditation to get caught in such a materialistic view of these practices. Modern Western thought advocates a strong allegiance to rational, conceptual mind. From this vantage point, it's hard to view thoughts as anything other than cold hard truth. When practitioners want to be told what to feel—because they are unable or unwilling to have their own experience—practice remains on a purely conceptual level.

As Yoga and Buddhism take root in the West, the occidental mind-set develops new relationships to spiritual practices transplanted from the East. We have no room in our cultural paradigm for myth or magic and this is precisely what pilgrimage requires in order for the transformation to occur. You have to step outside your current paradigm in order to adopt a new view. Because a new perspective is what will change your mind. You can't solve a problem using the same logic that created the problem. This requires that you learn to tolerate uncertainty and fear.

For some, staying on the surface of a spiritual path is enough. Many people want to learn to relax and de-stress or get fit and healthy, and these practices—yoga asana, pranayama, and sitting meditation—can help achieve that. But it is a travesty to present these wisdom teachings exclusively from this perspective and to assume that their worth stops here. And this is largely what a consumer culture has advertised. "Do these practices," it says, "and your life will get better."

But if you practice yoga[2] with the mind-set of a pilgrim, with devotion and dedication and discipline, that campaign slogan is a misrepresentation. There may be phases of the journey that feel messier than before you began. This is part of the path. It may get better at first; it may not. But your life will get more real—more honest.

I don't want to scare you off, but in order to uncover the brilliant jewel within, there may be some crusty layers of mud to chip away. The gift of these practices is that they give you practical tools to do this. But the work must be done. And it is not always fun or easy and some days you may wonder why you started in the first place. It is an essential part of the journey, and just like Naropa being tested by his teacher Tilopa, it will prepare you for the awakening of insight.

Chögyam Trungpa Rinpoche said:

We have a fear of facing ourselves. That is the obstacle. Experiencing the innermost core of our existence is very embarrassing to a lot of people. A lot of people turn to something that they hope will liberate them without their having to face themselves. That is impossible. We can't do that. We have to be honest with ourselves. We have to see our gut, our excrement, our most undesirable parts. We have to see them. That is the foundation of warriorship, basically speaking. Whatever is there, we have to face it; we have to look at it, study it, work with it, and practice meditation with it.[3]

Who Is a Pilgrim?

What is the difference between a pilgrim and a refugee? What distinguishes a pilgrim from a holiday maker? How can we discern between wayfarers, nomads, immigrants, flâneurs, expats, travelers, exiles, emigrés, deportés, wanderers, or yogis?

I'm particularly interested in Woman as Pilgrim. Journeys to or through the East were once the exclusive domain of men. What limitations and advantages arise for women as pilgrims in the context of patriarchy and organized religion?

Gaining access to spiritual teachings has not always been easy for women. Practices that are au courant these days—herbalism, astrology, divinations, sacred rituals—would once have earned a woman the title of Witch, along with a death sentence. What makes pilgrimage so powerful now—especially for women—is that it is fully accessible. There is no prerequisite, no fee for entry, no male escort required. In an era when sacred feminine wisdom is bursting at the seams to show herself, pilgrimage for women is like having the master key. You can open the front door to Shiva's abode.

The first Western woman to journey to the East was probably Alexandra David-Néel, and she had to disguise herself as a man to do it. Her memoir, *My Journey to Lhasa*, is one of the great pilgrimage stories of our era—please go read it if you want inspiration.

Tenzin Palmo, an English woman who spent twelve years in a cave in the Indian Himalaya, (read the whole story in *Cave in the Snow* by Vicki Mackenzie) asked her teacher Khamtrul Rinpoche why he thought there were not more female incarnations of Buddhist teachers. He replied:

> My sister had more signs at the time of her birth than I did, and when she was arriving everybody said, "Wow, this must be some really special being coming." But as soon as she was born, they said, "Oh, we made a mistake!" You see, if she had been male, they immediately would have tried to find out who this child was, and he would have been given a very special kind of upbringing. Because she was only female, she was not given a chance. She had to marry and so on. This was the problem, that even if you came back as a female it would be very difficult to receive the kind of training and opportunities you could get as a male.
>
> (*Reflections on a Mountain Lake*, Ani Tenzin Palmo)

Even today this is still an issue. While many changes have been made by the Dalai Lama to improve conditions for nuns, the seventeenth Karmapa writes in from *The Heart Is Noble*:

> I think a note of caution is in order here. Although there may be aspects of Buddhist teachings that can help us in thinking more wisely about gender issues, I want to warn you against looking to Buddhist societies to provide ideal examples of healthy gender constructs and practices. You should expect to come across things you do not want to adopt for yourself. Not everything in Buddhist institutions is perfect, and this is certainly the case when it comes to gender discrimination.

Most of the world's religions have been founded by men. Most saints are men. Some of the world's women saints have been burned at the stake. There is little precedence for a woman going off on her own to seek enlightenment. It was the dangerous exception, and not the norm.

Someone who is a pilgrim at heart does not accept her fate without questioning whether or not it fits with her values. She may very well decide to start a family, but her path takes priority—even if her path is family life. Unwilling to settle for a superficially satisfying life, she is looking for meaning.

When you feel the call, it's hard to resist. It's equally hard to explain to those who don't feel it. I'm not sure if a pilgrim is made or born that way, but I do know that some of my closest friends have never in their lives felt the urge to pack up and head to the far reaches of the planet. Many, if not most, of them are content to live the traditional family lives that were expected of them.

A pilgrim is a rebel. She seeks to know the truth of her existence beyond the cultural ideals and habits. She yearns for a direct connection to the divine spark of life, unmediated by a religious tradition. She refuses to accept superficial explanations to life's biggest questions, and decides to go find answers for herself.

The Making of a Pilgrim

The first steps of my pilgrimage had parallels to Naropa's. I was a graduate student studying Buddhist psychology at Naropa University—named after the Indian saint—in Boulder, Colorado. While there, I was introduced to three threads of inquiry that would permanently alter my view.

In August 1992, I had my first meditation instruction with one of Chögyam Trungpa Rinpoche's senior students, attended my first yoga class with Richard Freeman, and started coursework toward my master's in Contemplative Psychology—all in the same week. These practices became my tools, my way of viewing the world. They eventually helped me come to terms with and manage the chaotic emotional baggage I carried around from my childhood. I had to first acknowledge, sit with, and then accept these difficult emotions, something I had never done. I had learned to write about my feelings in secret.

"Free writing" is something I've done since I got my first journal at age eleven. Having been raised in a family where feelings were not discussed, this probably saved my sanity. Years of pent-up emotions fill hundreds of notebooks now stashed in my storage shed. Before I started practicing yoga, meditation, and therapeutic ways to process emotions, writing was my only tool.

While at Naropa University I developed a more sane relationship with my mind. I learned that it is possible to tame the mind through sitting meditation, and to settle the subtle body through yoga and pranayama practice. Working with therapists and at my internship, I learned the power of talking about and reframing experience.

These three lines of inquiry reshaped my life and directed me to new horizons. They helped me develop confidence. I gained tools and strength to deal with my demons. It has become my life's mission to share these tools with those who might benefit.

I am not what you would call a "spiritual teacher" and have little particular wisdom to share. But I have made the journey, met the teachers, and discovered the practices. The journey has enriched my life. I hope it will enrich yours, too.

I first started this book as a memoir. I wanted to complain about the often difficult and bewildering journey and get sympathy for all the crap I had to go through. After fifteen years of living overseas and traveling from Kathmandu to Paris to Sri Lanka to Hong Kong to Cambodia to Vietnam to Bhutan and a hundred mini pilgrimages in between, I covered a lot of ground.

I spent a year practicing Ashtanga Vinyasa Yoga in Mysore, South India, and five months in retreat on a deserted island in Vietnam during the monsoons. I had my only pair of shoes stolen on the last day of the Kagyu Monlam in Bodh Gaya, just as I was about to board a January flight home to Colorado. I managed a yoga studio in what is arguably the most luxurious hotel in Hong Kong and spent six weeks prostrating under the Bodhi Tree while waiting for a work visa to grant my entry into Bhutan. There were strangely serendipitous meetings with high lamas and auspicious coincidences that led to mind-boggling good fortune.

And I had more devastating heartbreaks during this phase of my life than at any other. I probably cried every day for twelve years. It simply is not convenient to have a relationship with a Western woman who is so fiercely dedicated to obscure esoteric practices. Despite this fierce devotion, I also had an intense longing for an intimate relationship. I could not find a resolution to the situation—until I changed my mind-set.

Free and wandering through the land of the historical Buddha, or planted in domestic bliss in my home country? The choice looked pretty black and white to me. But an awakened mind-set allows for shades of gray and the possibility that sometimes there is no resolution.

Program or Pilgrimage?

What is the difference between a program and pilgrimage?

A program has clearly delineated segments, steps, or outlines. There may be things to learn and identify. There is a goal to a program—you finish the program. Whether it is advancing to the next practice, accumulating a certain number of requirements, or staying for a set period of time—like a traditional three-year retreat—a program has finite parameters.

Pilgrimage, on the other hand, has no such definite or definable goals. With pilgrimage, everything is on board, even—maybe especially—the trials and tribulations that seem to keep you from practice. The messiness gets included on the path, and may even be the path itself. It's like going out of your way to dance with your demons. Pilgrimage is a conscious embracing of all the fears and obstacles in your life.

During my graduate studies at Naropa University, we learned to distinguish process from content. In therapeutic work, healing lies not so much in the content of the dialogue as in the process itself—the relationship that is created through talking.

I think it is the same with the spiritual path. It's not the teachings themselves that have the power, but the process of engaging the practices. Content is five hundred-hour Yoga Alliance–approved Yoga teacher trainings. Process is pilgrimage—discovering how your life can be transformed through integrating what you learn. I feel strongly that the Earth's healing will evolve from the latter and not the former. With the wrong view, you can practice diligently for years without ever having a personal experience—just like erudite Naropa before he quit his job at the university to find a teacher.

Pilgrimage is being aware of a larger context of a spiritual path while having a personal experience. It necessitates a sense of self-reliance and initiative.

You could go on a pilgrimage with a teacher leading the tour. But even then, the teacher cannot instill in the student the sense of courage and adventure necessary to allow this change to occur.

A pilgrim is not relying on a guru to give her something she thinks she does not have. Instead, she follows the example of the Buddha leaving his palace, and looks for her own answers. Even if she has no idea what the questions are.

A pilgrimage is self-secret. The answers—and the questions—are withheld until you have the maturity to see them. You don't actually know what it is you are looking for.

The true pilgrim has reached a point where she is ready to embark on a deeper level of inquiry, and move beyond spiritual window-shopping. She is independent and self-starting and disciplined enough to set out on a path of unknowns.

You might not know what you need in order to change. At the beginning, you just know that you are suffering and that you are motivated to make serious inquiries.

This is a perfect place to start. And the following practice—free writing—will help you navigate the terrain.

Writing Practice

Writing saved my life. Maybe it will save yours.

At the end of each chapter you'll find writing prompts to integrate ideas discussed so that they become personal and relevant to you. Writing practice is a powerful tool to access the subconscious in ways that talking doesn't. Often I find myself writing things I had no idea I thought or even knew. It's as if emotions get dredged up from the depths to display themselves to my conscious mind.

Writing practice can help you to identify and call by name influences that undermine your intentions. Once you have this information, you learn to recognize what upsets your equilibrium and how you can work with these obstacles.

Here's how it works:

Using specific prompts, you do what is called "free writing," which is essentially stream-of-consciousness writing with a general focus or theme.

There are three rules:

1. Write by hand, with pen and paper, NOT on the computer.

2. Write without stopping or lifting your pen from the page—either for a fixed period of time, or for a predetermined number of pages.

3. Don't censor or edit while you write. Let anything come out, even if it is gibberish. If you lose your train of thought or don't know what to write next, then write, "I don't know what to write and anyway this exercise is silly and I bla, bla, bla..." Eventually something will come and you will get back into the flow. The thinking mind will try to sabotage your subconscious, which is where all your juicy ideas are. Let it all out, knowing that this is FOR YOUR EYES ONLY.

You can use this practice in different ways:

You can use it to "clear the decks" of your mind, wiping the slate clean after you've had an argument, for example.

You can target different patterns and habits, all with the intent to release blockages to creativity. Ask open-ended questions like, "How am I getting in my own way?" and see what comes out.

Incorporate this practice into your daily routine to stay in touch with your inner world—so you give your feelings and insights the air time they deserve.

Bookmark this page to return to if you need a reminder.

Do a fifteen minute free write using the following question as a prompt.

> What is my story? (We'll come back to this particular writing exercise in chapter 4 so keep it handy.)

2

When Crisis Calls

⌒⌒

The Choice

There is a moment in every life when you realize you're at a turning point. Circumstances dictate that you make a choice, and by choosing one direction you irrevocably give up your chance at another. Forever.

I encountered such a moment when, instead of settling in to a traditional career as a mental health professional after my graduate studies, I flew to Mysore to study Ashtanga Yoga with K. Pattabhi Jois.

I was obsessed. Discovering Ashtanga transformed my inner world so completely that I had reoriented my entire life around the practice. My whole daily schedule revolved around accommodating practice: two- to three-hour practice sessions, early-morning meditation, weird dietary habits, jobs that allowed me to leave precisely at 4:30 p.m., so I could make it to the studio for the 5:00 p.m. Mysore class. I couldn't socialize with my old friends because our rhythms just didn't match. Traveling to India was an obvious next step.

But I hated India at first. I didn't understand it. I felt lost and vulnerable and alone. I couldn't wait to go home. Just because something is obvious does not necessarily mean you will enjoy it, or that you will be able to integrate the experience seamlessly into your life.

Suffering

The first noble truth Shakyamuni Buddha identified was the truth of suffering. We suffer when we don't get what we want. Then we get what we want and it gets taken away. Or we get what we don't want. These situations are not in themselves a problem—it is possible to accept life's hardships and move on. But most of us humans add another layer to life's pain—we resist it. We suppress our pain, or we act it out, or we ignore it completely, so that we end up carrying around heavy old baggage for the rest of our lives.

We suffer when we don't relate to the pain of life cleanly. We get attached to our view of how things should be—or how we ourselves should be—and then struggle when things don't go the way we want.

When you take the first step on a pilgrimage, you put your life in the hands of some inner, or higher, wisdom. You enter the unknown, prepared to face suffering directly. You finally admit that you cannot control outcomes, and surrender to the process of becoming who you truly are. You accept that there is some divine purpose to your life even if it is as simple as tending your own garden. It may not be as grandiose as the plans you had laid out for yourself, but it is your unique gift to offer the world. So there is a huge amount of trust involved, and a willingness to be with whatever arises along the path.

My belief is that this organic process of confronting ourselves is what creates depth and meaning. If you follow a prescribed set of rules set out by an organization, then the spiritual path becomes just another item on a daily to-do list, or a set of guidelines to follow. The intention of this book is to show how a shift in attitude—taking personal responsibility for your path—can create a new understanding of what it means to practice a spiritual discipline, and help you create your own unique experience.

As Chögyam Trungpa Rinpoche put it:

> Despite the clarity of the teachings, we often lose sight of this essential aim of eradicating mental poisons and self-clinging. In fact, instead of eliminating those poisons, we often end up increasing them. For example, people that practice the dharma have a tendency to gather together and organize themselves. They create institutions, dharma centers, and monasteries that can quickly become banners proclaiming their self-importance. "We are this. We are that. We are Nyingma! Kagyu! Geluk!" People in these institutions nominate someone to be president, secretary, and treasurer. These officials can easily become proud of these titles. Gradually, their activities come to be at odds with their original purpose.

Mindfulness and awareness practices provide techniques to help you get present—not so that you can earn bragging rights for the sublime quality of your meditation practice—but so that you can tune in to the wisdom and compassion that will guide you to follow your life's path.

If the intention of meditation practice is to tame the mind, pilgrimage gives you the opportunity to test the strength of your practice by turning up the heat. This forces you to confront situations that test your resolve—and the strength of your ego—to stay present in the moment. It's a bit like a large-scale science experiment. What happens to your state of mind if you take away all familiar reference points, disrupt your routines and expectations, throw in a few catastrophes?

Expecting Results

Every so often I get an e-mail from a student who has hit a road block and feels like giving up. A dedicated practitioner of both yoga and meditation wrote recently: "I've been hit by a strong dose of doubt about the path, meditation, Buddhism, self-help, spirituality… I'm fed up. At the moment, I just want to give up and be 'normal' again… Why bother?"

Just because you practice a spiritual discipline, it does not mean life will always go your way. Practice is merely the entryway into learning to grow from the experiences life tosses at you. It's not a remedy, but rather a tool.

Practice, if it is approached seriously, introduces you to your aloneness. Since the bulk of modern culture proposes everything under the sun to deny this fact of existence, continuing to practice is a defiant step against the standard view.

If you feel like giving up, it implies that you are trying to get somewhere. The truth is that there is no goal. And isn't this really what makes us unhappy? Thinking that we have not reached our goals? We want happiness, success, abundance, love, recognition, and when we feel we don't measure up against our goals, we suffer.

Rather than giving up, surrender your expectations. The true prize, if there is one, is the ability to be okay with whatever arises. This takes practice. By giving up the goal, instead of giving up the practice, you might even surpass the goal and make other, wonderful discoveries.

Essentially there is no path other than a commitment to live with authenticity and integrity, and no other goal than to live in the present moment.

Point of No Return

Five months after I returned from my first trip to India, while I was in between jobs, homes, continents, and boyfriends, my

beloved grandmother's health started to deteriorate. She had kept
her cancer secret for the first four years, until it was no longer
possible to hide. I strangely admired her approach—her feeling
was that if it was time to go, then so be it. She wasn't afraid of
death. She'd lived a rich life with many close friends and had
traveled all over the globe. I guess after you've done all you want
to do, there's no reason to fear.

I asked if I could stay and help make Toppy's transition easier
when the time came.

"Go live your life," she said to me. "I'll call you when I'm ready."

She preferred to enjoy her last days on earth in her quiet
way, keeping a simple routine at her Florida home: peanut butter
sandwiches and Kool menthols and long walks on the beach. Happy
hour precisely at 5:00 p.m. She never once went to see the doctor.
As she liked to say: Thy will be done. And I said: Fair enough.

When it was time, I went. Evenings we sat on the porch
drinking cold white wine in between bites of cocktail shrimp
while the sun set on the smooth Gulf of Mexico. Gentle waves
lulled the snow-white sands to sleep as the sky turned pink and
orange and gold. We listened to Billie Holiday and Glenn Miller
and sometimes turned on the Lawrence Welk show. She told me
stories.

She reminisced about meeting her father's close friend Charles
Lindbergh when she was a girl and signing her autograph on his
airplane. Her father was her hero; he piloted the first commercial
airline route for Pan Am, from Key West to Havana. When Toppy
was sixteen, she and her mother came home one day from a trip,
interviewing colleges. Her father did not greet them at the door
when they returned home, as was his habit, so Toppy went to look
for him. She opened the door to his study just in time to watch him
pull the trigger of the pistol in his mouth.

I could imagine how she felt in that moment. When she died, for me, it was like losing an organ. Toppy was my lifeline during adolescence and had been there for me faithfully my whole life. She waited up for me on high school graduation night, not to punish me, as others did, for coming home at 6:00 a.m. with my best friend's boyfriend, but to meet my defiant gaze with tenderness and to ask if my heart was troubled. No one ever asked me that, much less listened to my response.

I was so unhappy. Mostly, I was angry. I needed a stable home base.

I learned of my parents' divorce the day before I started junior high. In the 1976 middle-class suburbs of Washington, DC, where we lived, divorce was unheard of. I fully believed it was my fault—leaving me with a tinderbox of confused feelings.

That fateful night after graduation was the straw that broke my mother's camel's back, and the next day I was asked to leave the house. Set loose at sixteen. Decades later I still struggled with issues of self-esteem that often spiraled into depression. My relationships suffered. I'd beat myself up with each breakup, and relive the painful feelings I felt on that evening at age eleven when my known world fell apart. I kept trying to make it right and got more depressed each time I failed.

But I felt my grandmother's love. During my first two troubled years at Florida State University, I ferried my kittens from Tallahassee to the Florida panhandle almost every weekend just to walk the beach with her. I had fallen into a deep depression, fueled partially by a cocaine habit. I had a group of admirers, all coke dealers, who fed me a steady supply of the stuff. I couldn't ever sleep, or eat—all I did was study. I went to my grandparents on the weekends to get some ground under my feet. Toppy answered me patiently each time I asked her for details about my parents' divorce.

"Why did my father leave us?"

"He didn't want to go," she would repeat. "He loves you."

I tried hard to believe her.

Toppy's last days passed in a bright haze. A stroke finally confined her to bed, and she wafted in and out of consciousness. I fed her ice chips, wiped her hot forehead with cool towels and changed her bedsheets. I practiced yoga every morning on her Astroturf balcony four floors above the gulf, and escaped into the pages of *The God of Small Things* when I got overwhelmed by the specter of death.

I waited. But she had already taken her last beach walk and I needed to go back to work.

The last thing she said to me as I said good-bye was, "Hold me." I did, for a long time.

She died a few days after I returned to Colorado, on May 31, 1998. Later that afternoon, my boyfriend came over and told me about his new fiancée.

My anchor line snapped; I was adrift at sea.

The Right Map

Perhaps a spiritual journey is about making peace with your circumstances, even when life doesn't go the way you expect. Trying to follow someone else's path is frustrating at best. At worst, it prevents you from realizing your own dreams. To follow your calling and fulfill the mission you were brought here to complete, you may need to let go of preconceived notions of what your life should look like.

Admittedly, this can be painful. I've learned that in order to respect myself, I need to honor my quirky choice of lifestyle and accept that some people may judge me. But that's their problem, not mine.

Pilgrimages are custom made, and the demons you confront are yours alone. Your pilgrimage will look like no one else's.

Just because you make a choice and take a leap—it does not mean you will automatically be on board with your new decision. You may have huge resistance or regrets. You may face insurmountable obstacles. You may wish to run back home to your safe world—any world, even if it wasn't that safe.

I was raised at the tail end of an era that had clear ideas about how a woman should live her life. According to that view, the worth of a woman's life depended upon marrying well and having children, then nurturing said husband and children until death or divorce do you part. I'd never known any woman who did it differently. All the women I knew were, or would be, or had been married. And no matter how I tried, or wished or prayed, my life was not going in that direction. I felt like a total failure.

It became painfully obvious that family life was not my path. While my girlfriends were busy starting families, I was increasingly obsessed with yoga. Until that point we had shared goals and dreams, but with no cookie crumbs and plastic dinosaurs on the back seat of my car and no husband anywhere in sight, my life was taking a different, and unknown, direction.

On my thirty-fifth birthday, as I was driving to teach a class at the yoga studio, I passed a huge speed limit sign on the highway.

"Thirty-five," it glared.

"Why don't you add, 'AND STILL SINGLE'?" I screamed at it. I broke down and sobbed at the stoplight. It was 6:30 a.m.

Something had to change. Rather than accompanying my married girlfriends on playdates, trying to fit in a family culture where I did not belong, and where I might easily die of depression, I had to come up with a new map.

I dove into academia—got accepted into a PhD program, studying religion, psychology, and social change. My new status as a doctoral student made me eligible for a coveted position in my field that had presented itself. Immediately following my entry into graduate school I was offered an internship at UNESCO in Paris, for which I could earn credit toward my doctorate.

UNESCO
March 2002, Paris, France

I used to have heart pangs when I thought of Paris—longing so deep that I had physical pain in my chest. I had finished my undergraduate degree as a French major at the American University in Paris, and still felt ambivalent about trying to live the American dream—which, after living in Paris, had lost its appeal. I had a romantic image of Parisian life that I couldn't seem to shake.

My internship was in the newly created Department of Interreligious Dialogue at UNESCO, that noble institution with the greatest mission statement on earth:

"Since wars begin in the minds of men, it is in the minds of men that the defenses of peace must be constructed."

Most of the thousands of applications it receives each year are refused, so I thought: *This must be something special.* The twin towers had come down just a week before I received my acceptance letter, so I was ready to do my part for world peace.

I was so disappointed by what I found there.

Piles of useless paper clogged the desks, lined the halls, and filled offices and entire storage closets of the UNESCO headquarters. I met so many brilliant creative people at that institution—people losing their vision, through having their dreams suffocated by this paper. The mission statement is formidable and attracts great thinkers and leaders, but the formalities and limited reach of the organization never seemed to allow many of these people to actually put their great ideas into practice. Here I was making a political statement, leaving my country to the invading wolves after September 11, offering myself to the benefit of humanity and world peace, and they couldn't even manage to find me an empty desk.

Our department's mission was to promote cultural interaction between representatives of all religions in hopes of showing the world that we could discuss our common interests despite our uncomplementary faiths. The problem was that no one could agree on what that meant. I spent my entire internship deciphering, translating, and transcribing (on a ten-year-old dysfunctional computer that broke down every other day) the results of a survey that had been conducted ten years earlier and which was meant to be the basis for the functioning of the new department. I moved my office four times in three months. Meanwhile, inter-religious dialogue was not happening, anywhere.

When I learned the Dalai Lama would give teachings in Paris, I proposed inviting him to attend an interfaith conference we were organizing, and my supervisor looked at me, baffled.

"Mais non, c'est impossible."

China would never allow diplomatic relations between a United Nations organization and the political leader of Tibet, even if he was the religious head of Tibetan Buddhism. I felt like quitting right then and there.

But I had a reason to stay for the moment. Rumor got out that I taught yoga, and someone asked me to offer a class during the lunch hour. There was a basketball court in the basement, and so on Wednesday afternoons I had a captive audience of eager United Nations ambassadors, diplomats, and policy makers performing sun salutations at my command. At least I could get these people moving, even if I was unable to lift my department out of its stagnancy.

I realized that this was where I could actually help the world; not on a theoretical level through creating policy and implementing new administrative procedures, but through the practice of teaching yoga to individuals, one by one. I had found my niche, through the back door, or rather, in the basement.

Accidental Pilgrim

Sometimes I think pilgrimage is an accident, something we label after the fact. We head in the direction of something we think will solve all our woes, and BAM, we get dysentery, or divorced, or depressed, and end up doing something else entirely.

Or we get a French Tax Bill.

I taught private yoga lessons all around Paris for a couple of years after my internship, and following bad legal advice, made the decision to declare my wages as income from a solo corporation. I had to do things legally, as I needed the visa to be able to stay. When I finally realized what had happened, it was too late. What I owed in taxes starting the third year would in essence prohibit me, forever, from earning a decent living.

The worst part about going against the grain and choosing to pursue a spiritual path, or even adventure, over a traditional lifestyle is that you have few to cry to when the going gets tough. Even if they do empathize, no one really gets it. Few can advise you.

It was a bittersweet moment for me: I had created a thriving yoga community, but to keep it going was beyond my capacity. I was frustrated that I couldn't take it to the next level. As much as I hate to admit it, I suppose it came down to this: I needed a husband to survive Paris. If I had, like several of my yogini girlfriends, married a man from the European Union, I might have avoided the tax mess.

It would have solved the problem of working papers, and greatly assisted my morale. Alas, apart from my Turkish boyfriend—who was already married—I had no prospects.

Paris was a defining moment because it was where I started teaching yoga full time—and making a living. I hosted Richard Freeman for his first workshop in France, and I felt grateful for the opportunity to help establish an Ashtanga community there. But my work was finished.

Teaching yoga in Paris had not been my plan, but what plans ever are really planned? We may label something a failure, but this is how we sow the seeds of pilgrimage. Life intervenes to redirect us, up the ante, and test our mettle.

This is the point at which I found myself in the summer of 2003.

I had to move on. A friend in London proposed that we open a yoga studio together. After a few weeks of negotiations, the contract fell through. That's how I found myself, one sweltering August afternoon, lounging on Hyde Park lawn under the shade of an oak tree, contemplating my future and desperately trying to come up with a plan.

As my meditations deepened, something shifted and a small voice said, "Why don't you go to Mysore?" It was my own.

I'd sworn after my first trip to India, seven years earlier, never to return. But my yoga teachers were in Mysore, and I needed guidance. Previous experience had shown me that when in doubt about what to do, the best thing was to dive into practice.

I had no idea what I wanted, only a vague hope of "deepening into yoga practice" fueled by the disintegration of my life in Paris. I needed to allow that disintegration and see what was on the other side.

Crisis or Opportunity?

So it was that at age thirty-eight I moved to South India for a year to study Ashtanga yoga.

In Mysore, I rented a big old house and a beat-up moped. Every morning at 5:00 a.m. I saluted the sun and stood on my head. Every afternoon I hosted a wanton mix of students at my home for a class on yoga philosophy with Acharya Shankaranarayana, a Sanskrit scholar.

I dodged cows and Tata trucks on my scooter and hung fresh garlands of jasmine over my doorway. I practiced pranayama three times a day, every day. Afternoons I got out my watercolors and made a big bright mess. Every evening, after meditation, I sat on my front step eating papaya and curd under the gently swaying palm trees and contemplated how bizarre, and how utterly right this choice had been.

I learned to relax that year. I became softer. I learned to breathe deeply and to keep a strict discipline. I finally learned to silence the constant self-doubt that was an heirloom from my chaotic childhood. I started to paint. I earned a teaching authorization that gave me confidence to pursue my passion further. Suddenly I could travel the world and make a decent living doing it.

When I stopped trying to fit myself into others' versions of how I should live my life, I relaxed profoundly. I followed my heart to what brings me happiness: yoga, writing, art, and traveling in Asia. And while I was busy doing what I love, I found a community that shared my passion. I found my tribe. Rather than playing tagalong with my girlfriends' families, I had created my own. I also learned to love India.

I suppose it is the transitions that define us—how we move from one situation to the next. Moments of crisis invite us to take a deeper look at what's not working in our lives and to reset our course. Once you accept and open to change, you free up your critical thinking to pursue different options. Rather than viewing crisis as a problem to be solved, you see the possibility for a new beginning.

That year in Mysore was a turning point, where I developed a discipline that has become an integral part of my life. The experience showed me a key to discovering a glimpse of true happiness, maybe for the first time in my life.

Writing Practice: The Right Map

Use the following questions as prompts. Do a fifteen minute free write using each.

- If you could change one thing in your life, what do you wish you could change?
- How have you been trying to fit into someone else's version of who you should be?
- Where have you gone off course?
- How can you live your life as a pilgrimage or sacred journey?
- What would it take to create a sense of sacredness in your life?

3

Preparing for
the Journey

The Path of Yoga

If pilgrimage is a spiritual journey, then it helps to have a map—it helps to know where you're going. Practice is that map. It is difficult to see yourself clearly without a formal discipline to observe your tendencies. Transformation occurs not in denying or resisting these tendencies, but in accepting and allowing your particular style to manifest. Once you can clearly identify your ways of manifesting in the world, you no longer need to compulsively act out unconscious patterns. You can make intelligent choices in your life. You learn to avoid the pitfalls of destructive habits and instead listen to the guidance of your heart. This helps you to establish a connection to your inner wisdom.

These days there are many different schools of yoga and if you are looking for the right one, you will have some research to do. But apart from the style of yoga you practice, I think that it's more important to find a teacher that you resonate with. I happened to get lucky: the first yoga class I ever attended turned out to be with the right teacher for me. I never bothered looking at any other types of yoga because I trusted my teacher. The whole situation at the yoga studio resonated on an intuitive level. And I loved

Ashtanga Vinyasa Yoga. But that may not be the case for you. It's worth taking a few classes to see what feels right for you.

On the surface, the path of Ashtanga Yoga is a simple way to maintain physical, emotional, and mental health. Beyond that, it is the foundation of a spiritual path that people have been following for centuries. These tools provide a way to reframe your experience so that your suffering eventually becomes the seed of compassion, which then shifts how you approach your world.

Patanjali's classical Ashtanga Yoga presents a step-by-step path that leads the practitioner to increasingly subtle states of awareness, leading up to the experience of samadhi. The word *samadhi* is translated variously by different teachers: Georg Feuerstein uses the word *enstasy*. T. K. V. Desikachar defines it as, "complete integration with the object to be understood." Richard Freeman calls it deep meditation. B. K. S. Iyengar calls it union, and if you consider that we also translate *yoga* as *union*, you could say that samadhi is the realization of the yogic path.

It is important to note that the eight-limbed path of Ashtanga Yoga, known as Raja Yoga, or Classical Yoga, is NOT the same as Ashtanga Vinyasa Yoga. This is a confusing but very important point. Ashtanga Vinyasa Yoga is the system of physical postures developed by K. Pattabhi Jois in Mysore, South India in the early twentieth century.

The asana practice of Ashtanga Vinyasa Yoga follows a set series of postures, flowing together with vinyasa (linking) movements, performed with deep, rhythmic breathing (ujayi pranayama), internal awareness practices (bandhas) and focused gazing points (dristi). This combination of techniques engages body, breath, and mind, to help release and transmute stagnant energies.

Ashtanga Vinyasa Yoga shows you how to breathe deeply in a stable posture, and then, over time, to sit quietly. The slightest misalignment in posture can inhibit the free flow of breath, preventing the mind from resting completely. Learning to breathe deeply not only relaxes the body, but also helps focus the mind. Eventually, the physical body becomes pliable enough to sit still for extended periods and settle into deep meditation.

Ashtanga yoga in the classical sense is a road map: a step-by-step process of preparing the body and mind to arrive at a state of awakening, as outlined in the Yoga Sutras of Patanjali. In this foundational text on yoga philosophy, only one yoga posture is described: that of sitting still for meditation. But there is not much guidance for developing a daily practice in the Yoga Sutras—it is more of a philosophical treatise. This is where Ashtanga Vinyasa Yoga comes in handy.

Ashtanga Vinyasa Yoga—the practice that you might see in yoga studios today—comprises two of the eight limbs of classical Ashtanga yoga—asana and pranayama. The primary series is the first set of postures given to students when they begin Ashtanga Vinyasa Yoga. The practice starts with sun salutations, then standing postures, then an array of seated postures, and a cool-down sequence at the end. The whole practice takes about two hours, start to finish.

You may begin yoga simply because you want a healthier body, or a way to work with stress. That's fine. Yoga practice cleanses, tones, and purifies the organism on many levels: muscular, endocrine, skeletal, respiratory. Eventually you learn to work with subtle energies to access more refined states of awareness. So there is much more to work with than is presented in most studios today.

You start by working with the grossest levels in order to affect (over time) the subtler levels. So on your first day you may notice changes such as sore muscles and a sense of relaxation. With practice, you may notice yourself standing and sitting up straighter, with a heightened awareness of your breathing and your thought patterns. Eventually the body's systems begin to shift into balance, allowing deep breathing that clears away blockages in the subtle channels. This allows the mind to settle deeply so that meditation becomes a real possibility.

But you don't need to know any of this. It happens naturally with practice. Once the breathing slows down and deepens, the mind follows suit and you begin to notice subtleties of awareness that were previously unrecognized, below the surface consciousness. You begin to tune in to a deeper level of awareness. This is when things get interesting, because you begin to see how your habitual patterns may or may not support your intentions in life. Once you can see the pattern, then you can do something about it. But not before.

Do You Need a Teacher?

You can start practicing yoga or meditation pretty much on your own these days. Pick up a book or video, and you can piece together a home practice. So at a certain point the question arises: Do you need a teacher to follow a spiritual path?

Many of us in the West lack experience when it comes to relating to a spiritual teacher. On the one hand, you can discover spirituality through developing a contemplative practice such as yoga or meditation. These days it is easy to find guides who will show you these practices. With dedication, the practice will shift your perspective, allowing your inner wisdom to take root. So on one hand, you don't really need a teacher.

Some practices require a teacher to give permission—or transmission. In the Vajrayana path of Buddhism, a teacher is absolutely essential.

So in a sense, both are true:

1. We have all the answers inside.
2. We may need the help of someone who has already realized this to help us see it in ourselves.

There are dangers to both sides.

If you don't have a teacher, you may end up overestimating your progress, resulting in an inflated ego. You could spend a lot of time being very lost, believing you are on the right track when in fact you have just transmogrified ego.

On the other hand, if you think that only a teacher can give you what you need, you may end up putting the teacher on a pedestal and following blindly, without ever really looking inside to find the source of your wisdom.

From a practical perspective, there are techniques to learn. A teacher provides instruction and guidance. To follow a path to wisdom, whether it is through yoga, mindfulness meditation, mind-training or esoteric visualizations, you need to know what to do. You need the detailed instructions for the practices.

Having a teacher to inspire and guide you along the path can save you a lot of trouble and time, and help you avoid pitfalls. Rather than reinventing the wheel, you benefit from the wisdom of those who have gone before you.

It helps to have support and encouragement—a witness to your journey who has been there before you. The path can be lonely and confusing, and a wise guide can help alleviate fears and confusion. While sangha and like-minded community can also provide some of this, a qualified teacher offers assurance you are on the right path and will mirror back to you when you stray from the path.

A teacher can:

- help you learn the technique;
- provide guidance along the path;
- give you detailed instructions of the practice;
- save you trouble and time;
- share wisdom of those who have already walked the path to help you avoid known pitfalls;
- offer support and encouragement;
- witness your progress;
- help alleviate fears and confusion;
- offer assurance that you are on the right path; and
- mirror back to you when you stray from the path.

Here's the thing: you already have all the answers. You have direct access to your inner wisdom. You just need to learn to listen to yourself. But (this is a big but):

BUT, it's this "you" that needs to be identified. This requires looking. It's not small self that has all the answers—intellectual knowledge will not take you all the way to wisdom. It's a matter of expanding the idea of who "You" are. A teacher can cut through and point directly to this You, so that you might get a glimpse of it.

Most of us have blocked access to our inner wisdom from disuse or active dissuasion from our caretakers growing up. The aim of the spiritual path is to clear away whatever obscures this wisdom and reconnect us with it. A good teacher is like a therapist (but is not a therapist) trying to talk herself out of a job—she shows you how to access your inner wisdom so you can have your own experience of it. It's about developing a relationship with your inner guide.

You may have different teachers as you evolve. Ultimately, success along the path is dependent upon the quality of the relationship with the teacher or teachers. You have to learn to be a good student. If you put the teacher on a pedestal, you reduce yourself to being an unworthy servant of this great being. I don't think this is the right attitude. Yes, it's important to respect the teacher and recognize the qualities s/he has, but you also have the seeds of these same qualities. This is the whole reason to be around an authentic teacher—to recognize that you have that same potential in yourself. You get to experience what happens once the seeds have grown into full flower through witnessing it in another being. Their simple presence can help you to hold your mind in a particular state of meditation.

There is an aura surrounding a teacher who has experienced profound insights. This can be a powerful teaching in itself. I've often had the experience of feeling the atmosphere shift around a realized teacher—similar to a change of weather. It can be palpable, and yet because most Westerners are not familiar with the phenomenon, it can sometimes be a bit distracting. People often confuse this type of "magical" display with the wisdom itself, and get starstruck—and stuck. This can impede a student's growth if she does not realize that she still has to do the practice herself. You can't rely on the teacher to do your work for you.

Meeting the Teachers

I stumbled into my first yoga class in 1992 with a teacher named Richard Freeman. His studio was approved by Naropa University, so I earned required elective credit toward my master's degree for my studies with him. Slowly, yoga practice—especially Richard's presentation of yoga practice—changed me. During his classes, Richard had a way of helping me access parts of myself that I had hidden away. I cried each and every time I attended his class.

Sometimes I simply shed tears of gratitude during the final resting posture while he played his haunting harmonium.

Sometimes I would touch something deeper and spend twenty minutes in racking sobs, sitting on the curb out in front of the studio until I could collect myself enough to drive home. I didn't know what was happening, but I did know that I was feeling stronger, more grounded, more sane.

I had so many years of pain and rage stuffed into my journals, or simply ignored, that were craving to be released, and yoga allowed that release. Those feelings needed a safe space, a caring guide, and a powerful vehicle to move forward—they needed permission to come out. But the funny thing was that often the feelings themselves were unknown. I frequently had the experience of working through an emotion during a yoga practice without even really knowing what the emotion was—like a half-emotion, or an almost-emotion, or something that might soon become an emotion but was still in its infancy. It was as if a whole layer of experience existed just under the conscious awareness, and the intense physical practice of Ashtanga effected changes working on this level. I had so much junk to work with—so much confusion from childhood—I took to that practice like a fish in water. I had found my ocean.

What I loved about Richard's teaching style was that he never pushed his own agenda on anyone. He shared the view of yoga in his quirky and hilarious way, and let his students work out what to do with it for themselves. He presented possibilities for his students and we either accepted the invitation or not. As a result, we had to test drive for ourselves, rather than being spoon-fed ready-made answers. The biggest lesson I learned from him was to trust myself.

Chögyam Trungpa Rinpoche[4] had already been dead for five years when I first met him—hard to believe, but it felt true. Even though I never met him during his life, I felt such a strong connection to his legacy that I felt as if I had met him. I read his books, practiced at the retreat centers he established, earned a master's degree from the university he founded, studied with his students and listened to his recordings—so I got a full download of his teachings. Also, it's said that mahasiddhas, highly realized masters from the Tibetan Buddhist lineage, don't die; their bodies perish but the mind-stream continues to be available to those who seek them.

Trungpa Rinpoche brought a whole new approach to Vajrayana Buddhism when he landed in the West in the early 1970s and left behind a thriving community. Vajrayana, or Tantric, Buddhism constitutes the Buddha's third teaching, and is an approach that takes direct experience as the object of meditation. Because of the potential to misunderstand the instruction, its methods are secret and only taught to practitioners who show maturity and devotion to the teacher who bestows them.

Chögyam Trungpa Rinpoche's genius was to find a way to present these teachings to Westerners, who often lacked the context from which the Vajrayana traditionally emerged. His message was the most honest and real that I had ever encountered; his teachings were about learning to accept yourself and your place in the world, using meditation as the tool.

His autobiography contains a story about him as a young man traveling with a group of monks in Tibet. When the group approached a village, they came upon a vicious dog straining against his chain, eager to attack. The beast drooled and bared its teeth, growling. As they approached, the chain snapped and the dog charged. Everyone in the party ran—most of them away from the dog. Chögyam Trungpa Rinpoche also ran—directly toward the dog. The mutt was so confused that he turned away and fled.[5]

Face your fears head on; that was the message. The basis of Vajrayana Buddhism is to take the phenomenal world itself as the means to wake up. No need to relinquish or revere anything. Use the messy details of ordinary life as a mirror to see into the nature of reality, and transform confusion into wisdom.

When I came across these teachings—shared with me by the original students of Chögyam Trunpga Rinpoche—my life took a turn. This influence, along with the intense yoga practice I was doing, forced me to take a hard look at myself. I started to see that—despite everything I believed—I was someone who was worthy of being loved.

And so are you.

Where to Find a Teacher

I hear Dharma students in the West sometimes complain that it is too difficult to meet an authentic teacher. If you don't make the effort to go find them, this is true. But having spent nearly two decades traveling around the world to study with my various teachers, I can tell you from experience that if you want to meet authentic teachers, you can. You have to make the effort. This is the point of pilgrimage.

Naropa spent twelve years following his teacher Tilopa, waiting for him to give him teachings. And Tilopa spent as many years eluding Naropa until he was ready. It's often said that when the student is ready, the teacher appears. Authentic teachers don't go out and solicit students. You have to seek them. Or perhaps you have to prepare yourself for the meeting.

This is where the word *discipline* comes from. Isn't it interesting that we tend to think of discipline as a harsh punishment for some infraction or disobedience, whereas a disciple was a follower of a teacher of wisdom. Discipline understood in that context might mean something like, "training with the teacher." Or perhaps, training the mind.

In the West there have been many scandals in recent years involving teachers who abused their position and created chaos within their community. It is normal to be a bit wary of jumping in to a teacher-student relationship. The Guru-disciple relationship is not a traditional part of Western culture. Without a proper understanding of the nature of the relationship, it can be fraught with confusion. This is why it is so important to be careful who you study with. If the teacher is unauthentic or confused, then you might end up confused, too.

So this question of how to relate to the teacher is quite important. Read *The Guru Drinks Bourbon?* by Dzongsar Khyentse Rinpoche for more on this. You have to keep your intelligence and discriminating awareness intact even as you put your faith in another for guidance. But I would say that more important than faith is experience. If you experience the teacher as someone genuinely looking out for your best interests, then spend time with him or her. If not, look somewhere else.

Ultimately an authentic teacher will teach you to develop an authentic relationship with yourself. Just as you trust your teacher, you start to trust your inner guide. You have to develop the ability to listen to your heart, which is the inner guru. At a certain point the practice itself becomes the teacher.

> Each person must find his or her own path. Nonetheless, seek guidance from wise and compassionate people and listen to them earnestly.
> —His Holiness the 17th Karmapa, Ogyen Trinley Dorje

Fear

How do you start where you are when you don't know where you are? Starting out on your journey can be exhilarating! It can also paralyze you with anxiety and self-doubt. What if everything goes wrong? What if you fail?

Maybe you know something has to give, and yet you don't quite know how to maneuver the passage. Or you are afraid to make a change. Perhaps you are reluctant to hurt those around you. Understandable.

Fear may be a constant companion on your journey. This is not necessarily a problem. The key is not to let fear make the travel plans. Fear can come along for the ride, but not lead the way.

Where Will Your Pilgrimage Take You?

You may have in mind a rough outline of the journey you'd like to take. Perhaps someone has told you about a retreat somewhere, or a program you'd like to attend. Maybe you'd like to close your boundaries and go into self-retreat at home.

Or you may not know where to start.

You can't really plan, or despite the title of this book, create a pilgrimage. Pilgrimage is seeking you. All you need to do is listen. That said, there are practical issues to address. Here's a list of things to start considering when making a preliminary outline of your journey:

- Do you have a destination in mind?
- What do you want to do? Practice? Study? Meet a teacher? Visit a sacred temple? Attend a teaching?
- How long can you take?
- How will you get there?
- What will you do with your home while you are gone? Can you find someone to rent your home?
- What would you need to bring?

- If you are traveling abroad, will you need an entry visa?
- If working abroad, will you need a work permit?
- Money: How will you support yourself?
- Health: Do you have insurance coverage? Are there health issues that should be addressed before going to a remote part of the world?
- Are there relationship issues to work out?
- What will you say to your family?

Armchair Pilgrim

Maybe you yearn for a transformative adventure, but circumstances keep you home-bound. No problem. Being a pilgrim is a state of mind.

There might be no actual journey to take—yet. Perhaps the scariest journey of all is that of sharing something of yourself and putting it out into the world for all to see. Or walking down the aisle. Or saying NO, once and for all.

> The real voyage of discovery consists not in seeking new landscapes, but in having new eyes.
>
> —Marcel Proust

Perhaps your journey is not something of your choosing—the world caves in and you must pick up the pieces of a shattered life. How you approach the journey is what will make it either a pilgrimage, or an escape.

If you are limited in your ability to trek across the globe on an adventure, there are still ways to embark on pilgrimage. Some of my best pilgrimages have been done in my own backyard. I throw a tent in the trunk of the car and head out to the desert, or the mountains, and isolate myself from civilization for a while.

Getting out of the city, leaving behind the society of people and turning down the volume can be a powerful form of pilgrimage. After being in nature for a period of time, you start to tune in to the subtle dynamics—the rhythms of nature. You start to develop a personal relationship to the natural world.

Or it could be as simple as committing to a daily solitary walk in the woods, or to a specific discipline of silent time on your meditation cushion. The point is to spend time with yourself, in direct relationship with the natural world. That relationship is your teacher.

It can also be inspiring to read about the journeys other pilgrims have taken.

Here are some of my favorite pilgrimage stories:

My Journey to Lhasa, Alexandra David-Néel
The Way of the White Clouds, Lama Anagarika Govinda
The Way of a Pilgrim, Author Unknown
Seven Years in Tibet, Heinrich Harrer
The Snow Leopard, Peter Matthiessen
Old Path White Clouds, Thich Nhat Hanh
Cave in the Snow, Vicki Mackenzie
Enlightened Vagabond, Matthieu Ricard

Most important is your intention and state of mind. You might start your pilgrimage within the four walls of your retreat cabin if that is what's available to you.

Here's how you might approach a domesticated version of pilgrimage:

- ❧ Develop a daily practice.
- ❧ Study with a teacher—live or online.[6]
- ❧ Read stories and visualize new horizons.

- ❧ Be open to new possibilities (try writing practice
  for this).
- ❧ Daily walk in nature—this is where you discover
  the unexpected.

Nature is a conduit. You can go seek out high mountains in the Himalaya, or you can supplicate the local nature spirits by simply asking for guidance.

Set your intention as you set out on your nature walk and practice noticing signs that arise along your journey. Pilgrimage is above all a conscious tuning in to a more subtle level of listening that will help you shift your perception and eventually your state of mind.

Writing Practice: Fantastorming

What preparations would you need to make for your journey? Brainstorm ideas that come to mind as you envision possibilities. This is just a preliminary "fantastorming" (fantasize + brainstorm = "fantastorm").

Write a bullet list of ideas based on the following prompts:

Who?
- ❧ Mentors?
- ❧ Guides?
- ❧ Travel companions?

What?
- ❧ How do you envision the days of your pilgrimage?
- ❧ Moving around?
- ❧ Practicing in one place?
- ❧ Alone or with a group?
- ❧ What kind of experience leaves you with a feeling of
  exhilaration?

Where?
- Volunteer organizations?
- Religious organizations?
- Retreat centers?

When?
- How far ahead do you need to plan?
- Do you need time to fundraise?
- How long do you want to spend on the journey?

How?
- Is support offered?
- Are resources available?
- Do you have any relevant skills you could share?

Why?
- What is prompting your journey?
- What are your concerns?
- What is your intended outcome?

4

Setting Your Intention

Your Life's Purpose

There is a brilliant talk by Eckhart Tolle that I often share at the retreats I lead, called "Finding Your Life's Purpose." In this talk he essentially outlines the whole point of meditation practice: to become aware of the moments when we are distracted by thinking and to return to an experience of being present.

This is your life's purpose: to be present and awake for what's happening now.

Why is this simple instruction so hard?

It's only hard because we learn to avoid pain. In attempting to avoid pain, we create all sorts of distractions that then have secondary effects, causing further suffering.

Eastern spiritual traditions speak of samsara, the endless cycle of conditioned existence that all beings go through until we see through the delusion. This is what hurls us humans through lifetime after lifetime of suffering until we work through our negative karma and stop causing harm. Samsara is the result of ignorance—the simple fact of not understanding how we perpetuate our own dramas.

Pilgrimage is about discovering how you create your own drama. The lessons you learn help change your thinking so you can stop creating more drama. Eventually, you don't have to do that anymore.

Out of the Cocoon

Chögyam Trungpa Rinpoche talked about the cocoon we build around our experience to protect ourselves from the pain of life:

"The way of cowardice is to embed ourselves in this cocoon, in which we perpetuate our habitual patterns."

You may notice this in your own life as rigid routines, lazy habits, and staying with familiar experiences that allow you to avoid growth. A cocoon is characterized by a walling off from the world, in order to transform into a new incarnation. But if you refuse to take flight with your new wings, you stagnate, and the cocoon becomes a dead end.

It's possible to be so terrorized about the feelings you want to avoid that you build thick concrete walls around you so as not to feel those painful emotions. When an attitude of self-protection becomes your habitual stance in the world, then it becomes your prison. You not only keep the scary demon feelings away, but you keep all feelings away (because you either feel or you don't) and this can block you from hearing what your heart wants you to know. Your heart may be yearning to write music. But if you were shamed by your third-grade music teacher for singing off-key, you might deny you want to write music (or paint, or write, or create a nonprofit, or design feather-and-sequin hooker heels) just to avoid the pain of confronting that old shame.

"When we are afraid of waking up and afraid of experiencing our own fear," Chögyam Trungpa Rinpoche says, " we create a cocoon to shield ourselves…"

There is a point where the comfort of the cocoon becomes more painful than the prospect of fear at what awaits out in the great unknown world.

This is the birth of a pilgrim.

Setting Your Intention

What distinguishes a pilgrimage from a holiday adventure?

Intention. The pilgrim sets out to seek change. Even if the destination is a secular one, if the intention is to set the stage for a transformation to take place, then the psychological shift has already started to occur.

A tourist is satisfied to return with some happy memories, some nice photos, and a feeling of relaxation. A pilgrim, on the other hand, is guided by something more mysterious and perhaps a bit darker. A pilgrim sets out in search of her demons.

Setting intentions is a subtle art. When you intend to do something, it gets slotted into your mental machinery as part of the program. That does not mean it will happen. Life may intervene and obstacles may get in the way. But the intention to do something lays the blueprint for it to happen in a more organic way than a decision. This brings up a question.

What is the difference between a decision and an intention?

An intention is an attitude that aims for a general direction. It is a mental state, and can adapt as circumstances change.

Decisions tend to be based on reacting to an external stimulus, and often grasp at a particular outcome. They are reactions to outer circumstances. They are often fixed and inflexible.

Intentions aim. Decisions grasp.

Decisions are flimsy. They can be made off the cuff, and dropped just as easily. Decisions proclaim: Right (fist pounding on table). That's it! It's decided. You make a demand on your experience to produce a certain result. You set a goal and commit to the long haul, whether or not your environment supports it as you move forward. When there are clear signs that it's the wrong road, some of us even feel better about forging ahead, as if extra suffering somehow makes our progress worthier. We think we are being good and disciplined as we struggle through the muck.

Intention has an open-ended quality; it's a general direction or theme you aim for. There is room to accommodate fluctuations and new information as your life unfolds. It is flexible. Rather than deciding on a course of action, you set an intention and simply learn to be present in full as that intention manifests.

Decisions are conceptual; intentions come from the heart.

How do you formulate your intention to go on a pilgrimage? At the end of this chapter, I'll invite you to set an intention for your journey that feels genuine.

Intention or Goal?

I make a distinction between intentions and goals. For me, intention is a larger view to work toward something. Once you have a clearly identified intention—for example, to be kind to people, or at least not to harm them—then you can break it down into smaller steps or goals. These you can think of as your daily practices.

A daily practice might be to say something kind to people when you first see them, or to offer a word of encouragement, rather than to immediately share your own experience. See what is up with them first. (If you don't already do this, you'll be amazed by the shift this small detail can make in your life.)

Intention is wide-angle vision, like when you turn the wheel slightly to steer in the right direction. It's more like an approach. If I intend to travel to Mount Kailash, then it's a possibility in the future even though I may have no idea how to do that yet. Then I might set a goal of learning how to get there.

So with goals, you identify a plan of action. Goals are like concrete steps to get from point A to point B. Identify which airlines fly to Lhasa by next Tuesday; an itinerary by October. Goals are hugely beneficial and important to create structure for larger projects. Once you get to point B, then you reevaluate the goals and current circumstances. Maybe you get to Lhasa and the roads to Kailash have been washed out. Then you may need to come up with other plans, all the while keeping your intention—the larger view of a journey to Mount Kailash—in the field of vision.

Goals are measurable. So if you fail to accomplish a goal, then you may be hard on yourself, or angry at others. This is why goals can so easily become ego's weapons—because you compare your vision to reality. Setting intentions allows for things to evolve.

When you hold your intention in mind, you can then identify the steps that will support your intention. These are called practices.

Then take action and do your practices. If you start practicing meditation—or anything!—five hours a day, I guarantee things will happen. If you don't have that kind of time, then start with five minutes a day. Regular, short sessions add up to change over time. Better to practice even a little bit every day, rather than a big chunk once in a while. Consistency over quantity.

So if you want to set out on pilgrimage, set that intention. Hold it in your awareness and listen to the ideas that arise. Make time to do your yoga practice and let that be your priority.

Energy flows toward your focus.

Begin or Recommit to a Practice

Practices are available everywhere these days—in studios and meditation centers, at conferences, in magazines and books and retreat centers. Your workplace might offer free classes at the lunch hour. You can Google esoteric Eastern practices and find teachings online.

But if you get spoon-fed by popular culture and rely on this as the source of your spiritual diet, then you might miss the depth or true purpose of these practices. Or you might get so excited by each new approach to meditation or form of yoga that you end up as a spiritual window-shopper.

Because of the plethora of approaches in the spiritual marketplace, it's possible to spend a lot of time (and money) creating the illusion of a spiritual path, without ever developing a personal relationship to these practices. Your personal experience is where the transformation happens. This is why pilgrimage is so important right now—it's how you develop your own relationship to practice.

What do you practice? Reconnecting with your inner wisdom, accessed by sitting still and observing the mind. This practice is simple—but not necessarily easy. Develop a regular practice of learning to ally with something other than the thinking mind. Practice allows you to cut through the onslaught of thoughts that regularly occupies the mind and check in with yourself so that you can hear that wisdom.

Awareness is only accessible in the present moment. The easiest way to access it is through coming back to the breath. A mindfulness practice like sitting meditation is essentially a tool to train the mind to be present. Concepts disconnect you from the present, so the practice is to learn to disidentify with concept and ally with the present.

Let Go and Allow for the Unexpected

The next step is perhaps the most important: to get out of your own way. This is where your intention gets plugged in to something larger than you. You are not the driver. You can set the course by visualizing your intention, but you have to eventually let go and give up the illusion of being in control.

Notice what moves you. When you have strong and unexplainable emotional yearnings, pay attention. They are your life force manifesting for you to experience. If you can't yet admit to yourself the life that calls to you, you may get messages to remind you.

This is perhaps the most important skill to have as a pilgrim—learning to let your intuition guide you. The more you practice it, the stronger intuition becomes. There is a certain skill in learning to ride that edge between holding a focus and allowing for fluctuations to arise. The same way you might hold a challenging yoga posture is how to approach the path of pilgrimage: not too tight, not too loose.

Too tight is being bound by earth, not allowing for the unknown to arise. Too loose is getting lost in space, fantasizing instead of waking up to the current reality. Learn to walk that razor's edge between the known and unknown worlds.

Open yourself to magic.

Write: Setting Your Intention

If an intention is the practice of training the mind to rest in the present moment, how do you set goals and make life plans?

Set aside at least an hour for this. You might want to go for a long walk first, holding each of these questions in mind as you walk.

Go back to "Your Story" that you wrote in chapter 1 and circle or highlight anything that feels charged, either positively or negatively.

Do a fifteen minute free write for each of the following questions:

- Where does your heart call you to go? (This could be a geographical place or a state of mind or a situation.)
- What would you like to grow out of?
- What would you like to grow into?
- How do you envision yourself in your ideal future?

Now write down your intention in one sentence. Memorize it.

- What is the intention of your journey?

Part 2

Phases of the Journey

Bangalore to Mysore
Tippu Express

I am squashed against the window by a large, dark man in polyester trousers who smells of spices and sweat. He's reading a book on breathing and yoga, in English. The train passes high over a drainage ditch, filled deep with opaque gray water, the surface littered with cartons, rinds, and greasy bottles. I look down and see a man stooping next to it, filling his plastic jug, for what, I wonder. The man next to me starts to discuss the benefits of "yoorine" therapy and wants to know if I have partaken in the occasion?

For the record, I have never drunk my own urine, or anyone else's for that matter. I inform him so.

I love the passenger train from Bangalore to Mysore. Not the Shatabdi Express, with its pseudo luxury, vinyl reclining seats, air-conditioning, dingy, curtained windows, and catered lunches. No, I prefer the slow trains: Tippu Express, Chamundi Express, Mysore Pass, where you can hang your elbow out the window between the dirty iron grates and breathe in South Indian suburbs. The acres of filth and rubbish, the clean clothes drying in the hot, stinking sun, just above the putrid, fermenting heaps of chicken and cow shit, flocks of goats, gangs of children and packs of dogs. Mothers clutching toddlers; toddlers clutching infants. Women washing dishes at the neighborhood pump, their saris hiked up between their thighs as they sit on their haunches. The heat and dust and rain. The smell of earth.

I swore during my first trip to India that I would never return. But things change. Life in Paris left me with a yearning for depth: for community, a teacher and disciplined yoga practice. Sure, we had a small community in Paris—a really nice one—but we were all so busy trying to make a living that it was hard to stay connected. Late nights in the big city tired me out. I need rejuvenation and a re-think about my life.

The scent of citrus suddenly permeates the air. I feel a tap on my shoulder and a middle-aged man from our crowded compartment offers me a section of his freshly peeled orange. He doesn't say a word, just smiles and shakes his orange-laden hand urgently, encouraging me to take it. I do, and smile back. As I eat, I think about the invisible thread that connects us all. Then I wonder when he last washed his hands. We don't look at each other again for the rest of the journey.

"Chai, chai!" a man exclaims repeatedly, galumphing down the aisle with his heavy load.

I love the simplicity here. The lack of choice. Not, "What kind of tea do you want?" But rather, "Tea is there itself. Do you want it or don't you?" At my request, Chai Man stops, puts down his stainless steel double-handled Thermos jug. He fills a small paper cup for me and I hand him a coin. It's spicy, the way I like it. I reach under my seat to get a packet of ginger cookies to dunk, and spill chai on my lap. The man next to me, I don't know whether out of kindness or irritation, gestures toward my cup. "Shall I hold it for you?" I accept gratefully and offer him a cookie once I have found them.

Outside on the planet a young couple strolls through a trash-strewn field. He's straight out of Bollywood, mustachioed and virile, carrying the toddler. She's in bright pink silk, fresh jasmine in her hair, flawless, as if they've been transposed here from a different time warp—the dimension where things are fresh, clean, beautiful, and pure. Instead of this land that has been used, worn, spit, shat, and yoorinated upon.

A pastel yellow butterfly, seemingly oblivious to this discord in the time/space continuum, floats gracefully in the petrol-fumed breeze. A rock path, dusty and desert-like: I think of Phoolan Devi, the Bandit Queen from Bihar, and her tragic triumph over the horrors of man and that brutal land. Still morbidly fascinated by the degradation she suffered at the hands of those outlaws who repeatedly raped her, and the strength she commanded to pull herself from victim of poverty (and gender) to become a member of Indian parliament in the late nineties and eventually a national hero. I wonder which is the greater motivator: love or rage? A wave of wild, raw power washes over me.

Halfway through the journey greenery starts to prevail. Deep, lush, green, as I've never seen elsewhere. Electric green. Blinding green. Coconut palms and long tall grasses, rice paddy and mango trees, and exotic pom pom bushes—huge blades of thick grass bunched and waving together with spherical pink-white flowers like a cotton candy explosion bobbing and bouncing just above the center of the whole beautiful thing.

So crowded, this land. Phenomena everywhere: animals, vegetables, and minerals. People: swarms of them. I suppose that's what made me think to bring condoms.

It's hot. So hot that I shiver and feel ice rushing up my spine. My loose cotton skirt sticks to me. My bare arms revel in the dirty breeze while layers of black accumulate on my skin.

The man with that cockamamie rice dish passes by in the train aisle. Puffed rice, onions, lemon, chilies, salt and some other ridiculous things mixed together to make a big sticky mess and give you stinky breath and fingers. Oh, and grated carrots, for god's sake. And the whole thing wrapped up and served in yesterday's dusty news. I fix my gaze firmly out the window as he passes.

Outside, a dark man, white T'd and turbaned, stands in his field, Madras-checked dhoti hiked up around his skinny legs. A cow, so white she's almost blue, elegantly picks at greenery under the palms in a coconut grove. Baby pigs, my absolute favorite. Nothing in the world can keep me from smiling when I see their little pug feet rushing, their snout noses to the ground, following the leader. Oink oink.

We pass Srirangapatna just after the Kaveri overpass, the last stop before Mysore. These are river shores where I can imagine Krishna playing with his gopis, the milk maidens. Idyllic groves nestled along the rocky coastline, neat mud houses with thatched roofs, absolutely timeless. I see the God Krishna hiding in the trees, waiting with his flute until the cowgirls are all bathing, with their saris tucked away under a rock. Then the Blue Rascal emerges to steal every last one, so that each young naked girl must approach and give him a kiss before he'll give her sari back to her. These shaded shores hold the history of ages, and the myths of eons. Proof that human folly will always be the same.

People appear on a platform, horns blare, brakes screech, and the train slows to a stop at Mysore.

5

Commitment

Mysore

Knowing what to expect made landing in Mysore easier the second time around. The *shala* (the traditional word for a yoga practice room) had moved since my first visit, and K. Pattabhi Jois's popularity had exploded. It was a drastically new situation.

I rented a room for a month in his old house, which now served as a boarding house for Ashtanga students. It was directly across the street from the new shala. Another change was having access to Internet, so it was easy to prepare my visit ahead of time, especially as a friend had secured the room for me before I arrived.

Mysore had become a mecca of yoga a century earlier when the Maharaja of Mysore requested yoga teachings from T. Krishnamacharya,[7] the grandfather of modern yoga, and his students K. Pattabhi Jois, T. K. V. Desikachar and B. K. S. Iyengar. Due to this royal patronage, a thriving yoga community had developed over the years, along with some highly specialized pandits who set up various schools. As a result, there is usually a large transient population of Western yoga students in this quaint South Indian college town.

I studied with K. Pattabhi Jois's grandson Sharath, who was also the Ashtanga lineage holder, a few blocks away in the same residential neighborhood as the main shala. I preferred the small classes—Sharath's twelve students to Guruji's eighty—and I had a good rapport with Sharath.

Sharath's class also started at a luxurious 8:00 a.m., rather than K. Pattabhi Jois's grueling 4:30 a.m. opening session. The weather in August, when I arrived, was balmy and dry and papayas were just coming into season. I met good people. My dark Parisian winter started to thaw.

I requested to study with one of my teachers, Acharya (*acharya* means *teacher*, and is used as a title of respect) Shankaranarayana Jois—with whom I felt a deep connection. Something about his presence always stretched my mind a bit, and pulled at my heart. I suppose this is how you recognize your teachers—they demand, and are granted, immediate access to your heart. I had met him on my first visit to India—he and his wife Vijaya had been a big reason for my return to Mysore.

There were only five of us studying yoga philosophy with him this time, with pranayama instruction immediately following. Acharya gave us each an individualized sequence of breathing exercises to do, based on our particular constitutions. Some needed more invigorating sequences to counter lethargy; some of us needed to relax. He stayed with us throughout the mid-day pranayama practice, sitting quietly in a corner of the room, observing, as we progressed through our breathing sequences.

I practiced the sequence three times a day: early morning before asana practice, midday before lunch, and evening as the sun set. The technique involved breathing in through one nostril and out the other, holding the breath for counts of thirty-two on alternate cycles. The work was painstakingly slow and subtle, and I had come to know parts of my lungs that I never knew existed. The effect on the mind was delicious. Blissfully calm and spacious. Like a holiday from chatterbox mind.

Ashtanga Yoga

Ashtanga in Sanskrit means eight limbs, and asana—the practice of physical yoga postures—is just one of those limbs. Yama and niyama, the first two limbs, deal with ethics and behavior—basically how to be a decent and disciplined person. Asana, from the Yoga Sutra point of view, means the posture of meditation. Popularization of yoga in the West expanded this term to include all the physical poses found in yoga studios these days.

But essentially, yoga is about learning to meditate by preparing the system, and then guiding the mind to stillness. Pranayama, the fourth limb, is about harnessing the power of the breath and putting it to use in the service of meditation. Pratyahara translates as "withdrawing awareness from sensory objects" and allows for undistracted focus. The last three limbs, dharana, dhyana, and samadhi, sometimes called samyama together, are essentially more and more subtle stages of meditation, culminating in a state of ultimate freedom from attachment to the conditioned world—the mukthi, or liberation all yogis seek.

On my first trip to India to study with K. Pattabhi Jois, I learned that these steps are the supposed background of the yoga practice, and yet I noticed that we never discussed them. K. Pattabhi Jois's famous motto advises that yoga is, "99 percent practice, 1 percent theory."

One day I found the opportunity to ask Guruji—this is how we referred to K. Pattabhi Jois—about it.

"If Ashtanga is for purifying the body, how do we purify the mind?" I said.

"Ashtanga yoga is for purifying mind," he said.

I wondered, if Ashtanga is about mind purification, then why did we emphasize the body so much?

Next time we had "conference" on the front steps of his house in Laxmipuram, I asked again, "Why so much emphasis on the body? Why don't we study the other seven limbs?"

"Asana is door," he said in his broken English, "then discovering other limbs."

So how does one do that? And how does the yoga practice as we know it today help facilitate this process of guiding the mind into stillness?

Training the Mind through Ashtanga Yoga

One simple place to start discovering the other limbs of yoga is by connecting the awareness to the breath, pranayama. Prana (also called *chi* or *lung*), the subtle and intangible life force in the body, rides on the breath. You can track the movement of prana by observing the flow of breath. You can experience this in yourself, and with practice it's possible to observe this flow in others as well. This is a great skill to have as a yoga teacher, for then you can help guide students to awaken areas of the body that may be asleep. The ability to observe subtle patterns in the body requires extreme sensitivity—you have to reduce external distractions in order to finely tune your awareness.

When you are able to reduce distractions, it is a sign that Pratyahara is developing. You shift your allegiance from external reference points to internal ones. It's like you finally are on the map. One practical way this might manifest is that you suddenly notice that you have moments of being completely absorbed in your practice, and not distracted by whatever else is happening in your environment. It's not just daydreaming—it's focus, magnified. You've probably experienced this before. It's what happens when you are so engrossed with something that "time flies" and you suddenly realize that you've been focused for a long period.

The last three limbs—dharana, dhyana, and samadhi—essentially convey the practitioner through a process of refining the awareness, with longer and longer periods spent in undistracted mindfulness.

So while the yoga practice as you may understand it happens on a sticky mat, with experience it can evolve into a stable seated meditation posture as the mind becomes increasingly settled. This is the most conducive environment for samadhi to arise.

This is why many people criticize the emphasis on the physical practice of yoga asana these days. Pictures of beautiful people doing fancy postures on social media really have nothing to do with yoga. The goal is not to perfect the postures; the goal, if there is one, is to tune in to a highly refined awareness. The practice is just a tool to help you do that.

So how does jumping around on a yoga mat get you there? You begin by bringing mindfulness and awareness to the process. Mindfulness is the faculty of not forgetting what to do and what not to do. It simply means recollecting what you are trying to do in the practice—remembering postures, breathing, and internal mudras.

But unless there is also some element of awareness, it's entirely possible to bypass this process of moving toward meditation and keep the practice on the purely superficial level. So you also add awareness, a big-picture view of what you are doing.

You observe the process of being mindful. According to Buddhist philosophy, it is this insight—the vipassana aspect of awareness—that cuts suffering at its root. So while mindfulness keeps you continually returning to the practice, awareness maintains an open inquiry into the nature of all that is unfolding.

The whole point is to be present in body and mind without distraction and without attachment. Right now. That is meditation. Rest in that experience for a while—say four hours—and you have samadhi, which some say is our natural state of being before we cover it up with endless distraction. If you continue to practice in a disciplined way, eventually you find your way home to a state of mind that is pure, unadulterated bliss. But even this is not the end goal—bliss is just a perk along the path.

Study

While there is wisdom in not over-intellectualizing practice, study can be helpful. Over the years it has helped me enormously to study the classic texts on yoga and meditation to formulate a map of the terrain.

In Mysore I attended classes with Dr. Shankaranarayana Jois—who reputedly was a distant relative of K. Pattabhi Jois, though I never confirmed this. Acharya was a Vedic astrologer and Sanskrit professor from Mysore University. Interesting note: the surname Jois indicates coming from a family of Vedic astrologers who practice jyotish. So apart from any blood relations, they are joined by family heritage.

Acharya taught the *Bhagavad Gita*, the *Shiva Samhita*, and *Yoga Sutra* to a small group of us on the concrete floor of his cool traditional South Indian house. We sat on straw mats and offered garlands of jasmine to Acharya, as we called him: teacher. His wife, Vijaya, started and ended each session with a beautiful devotional song.

Our classes on the *Bhagavad Gita* shed new light on the importance of nonattachment. Don't be concerned about the fruits of your actions, it counseled. The goal of the yoga is to just do something positive—to do your duty.

The human predicament is that our natural state of mind has been infiltrated by our distraction. You can't just wish your way back to wholeness. It's like if you find yourself a long way from home—you've got to start walking, or stick your thumb out, or—like Dorothy in *The Wizard of Oz*—click your ruby slippers together to get back home. You can't just sit around and hope you will find your way back, or you never will. You've got to act. Yoga practice is like clicking your ruby slippers three times—it's the vehicle. Done with sincerity and devotion and faith, eventually you will find your way home.

Study of the classical texts can help put the practice into context, so you have a sense of how it all fits together. See "Recommended Reading" on pages 233–234. Traditionally you would study directly with your teacher, going through a text and contemplating its meaning. However, these days many yoga teachers have never even heard of, much less read, the classical texts.

Translations also vary, so it can be helpful to look at several different versions to arrive at your own understanding. My favorite translation of the *Yoga Sutra* is by I. K. Taimni, and I also recommend one by Edwin Bryant. Georg Feuerstein wrote voluminously about the classical study of yoga and his books are highly recommended. With online study so readily available—and yoga becoming so mainstream—it is worth researching a quality online course to delve into the subtle aspects of these classics.

You may find opportunities to study at two hundred- or five hundred-hour teacher trainings. But my sense is that with the stated goal of "training teachers," there might be a tendency to rush through the study of texts. Depth of understanding comes from sitting with—and contemplating—these teachings, rather than reading them merely as a prerequisite for earning your teacher's certification.

The Inner Forms of Yoga

When you practice intense physical postures, as is the case in Ashtanga Vinyasa yoga, you challenge the organism to tolerate, and relax into, increasingly intense states of mind.

On a deep level, the Ashtanga yoga practice shifts the subtle body, balances and aligns it. Working with breath and postures clears blockages in the nadis, which are nonphysical channels of energy in the body, similar to the meridians of traditional Chinese medicine. Steady balanced breathing equals a steady balanced mind. But it takes a while—possibly years or lifetimes—to be able to maintain steady slow breathing while standing up with one leg behind your head.

The shifts that take place in the subtle body as a result of the Ashtanga practice serve as an engine for propelling you along the path of pilgrimage.

How does this work?

Yoga philosophy talks of granthis, or karmic knots, in the nadis that occur as a result of blockages—our unresolved physical, emotional, and mental baggage. This is what causes consciousness to stagnate at certain areas of our life—whether in our body, our relationships, our emotional life, or our thought patterns. They manifest as our blind spots, destructive habitual patterns or weaknesses.

When you move through the series of postures of the Ashtanga system, you stimulate various areas of the body at a deep level, and then intentionally breathe into these areas using the ujayi pranayama breath technique. So the concentrated breath gets directed to the areas of blockage.

Some areas are quick to release, and you might notice a greater physical ease after only one or two practices. But some knots are buried deeper, and tied up more tightly. These may take years to undo. The point is that the practice of directing focused, conscious breathing to the entire body has profound effects on your awareness. As a result, you may notice things coming to the surface—old memories, family issues, dreams—so that you can work with them. Obstacles that have held you back may grow huge as they take center stage long enough for you to be able to acknowledge, and then finally release them.

This is why it sometimes feels like things get messier before they get cleaned up. I get frustrated with modern media's insistence that yoga and meditation practice will make you relaxed and peaceful—it is not the whole story. The truth of the situation is that if you want peace, you must confront your demons.

Develop a Daily Practice

The sign of a truly dedicated practitioner is a self-guided practice. Tibetan yogis head off to their caves for decades at a time to experience isolation, which breeds self-reliance. Learning how to develop and maintain a meditation practice on your own takes perseverance, dedication, and patience.

How do you develop a daily practice? Like this: one day at a time, include short periods of practice into your daily schedule. It means getting on your yoga mat each day and/or your meditation cushion each morning. It means at a certain point you'll have to have a conversation with your family to let them know that this is something you are doing with your time, with your life. You'll probably want a teacher or at least a guide—a live person to relate to about the path. It means that you have made a choice to undertake a training of your awareness, which is unknown territory.

Many people will not understand your choice. This is part of the path: learning to deal with going against the grain of society's norms. Ironically, to make this shift, it helps to have a daily self-practice.

The beauty of Ashtanga Vinyasa Yoga is that the practice is self-motivated, so you get the direct experience of self-practice from day one. It may be easier to be led through a practice while attending a yoga class—you simply have to follow instructions. But when you are creating the experience yourself, you develop self-discipline and confidence.

It may be messy at times and you may wonder if you are doing it right. In my experience, the only way to gain true confidence in your practice is to muddle through it using your own GPS system.

It doesn't have to be Ashtanga yoga. But I think whatever practice you do—whether yoga asana from a different lineage or sitting meditation—has to be self-directed.

There are too many different brands of yoga these days to mention them all, but if you find an authentic teacher you like and trust, you'll be able to find a practice that works for you. I suggest sticking to a form of yoga that comes from a lineage rather than one that someone has recently invented, trademarked or franchised. Any form of yoga that comes from the lineage of Tirumalai Krishnamacharya—whose students included B. K. S. Iyengar, K. Pattabhi Jois, T. K. V. Desikachar, Indra Devi, and A. G. Mohan—is a good place to start. There are also other schools such as Kripalu, Sivananda, Satyananda, Kundalini, and many more. Many of the names commonly seen on studios in the West—Core Power, Vinyasa, Yin, Bikram, Power, Flow—are recent additions to the world of yoga and may not offer a complete approach to practice. That can be fine if you are seeking an entry point for your journey, but just know that there may be more on offer when you are ready to go deeper.

Only you know your body and mind as intimately as you do, so you are the only one who can read the signs. It's like training your ear to learn a new language—it's all gibberish at first, until you break it down, one syllable at a time. It's not something you can accomplish in a day or a week. It takes dedicated, disciplined practice, and time. It is absolutely sure that if you apply yourself, results will occur.

Each day when you get on your mat, you drop into your breath, making it regular and even. You drop into awareness of the bandhas, accessing a sense of grounding in the body, which then connects to the breath. As you move through the postures with these two features of breath and bandha engaged, you clear away the previous day's mental and emotional garbage. Over time, the effects are cumulative. What happens is a radical restructuring of the entire body-mind system. But it happens with just a few minutes each day on your yoga mat—like clearing out the cobwebs on a regular basis.

Dedication

Learning to maintain a meditation practice takes dedication. I remember the moment when the process clicked. I was rushing out the door to go teach an early-morning yoga class, feeling frazzled and late. It was midwinter in Paris and I had overslept. I was about to walk out the door without doing any practice whatsoever—I did my yoga practice in the afternoons—and I stopped myself.

"What are you doing?" I said to myself. "You are a teacher of contemplative practice, so go sit down and follow your breath before you teach a class. Do it now."

And I did. I sat for one minute and watched my breath settle down just a bit. I walked out the door in a new state of mind, confident that I had access to the state of mind I was about to go teach. That was nearly twenty years ago and I have almost never missed a day since. Even if I am rushing to an early-morning flight, I at least follow my breath in the taxi on the way to the airport. The thought of missing my morning meditation is like forgetting to brush my teeth—I would feel gross and vaguely antisocial for the rest of the day.

But it hasn't always been easy to become a daily meditator. At times, we all need a bit of support. It is enormously helpful to have a community of fellow practitioners, called sangha.

The beauty of meditating with a community is that the group energy serves as motivation to get on your cushion. This can be a weekly—or daily—group practice at a local community center.

It could be a retreat where you go totally off-grid for a week or twelve. Or it could be a program with a meditation teacher, weaving in sessions of meditation with teachings about the view of practice.

Group practice is incredibly powerful to help you establish—or reestablish—your balance. It's a great way to develop and maintain a meditation practice at the beginning. I think it's important to schedule sitting with a group on a regular basis, just to make sure you are keeping it real.

That said, when you are meditating by yourself, you get direct access without any distractions. It can be incredibly empowering to develop the personal discipline to keep your mind focused without anyone telling you how to do it.

This is what will strengthen your dedication and help you maintain a daily meditation practice. For this you have to allow for the possibility that—at times—you might get it "wrong." You might spend a full hour fantasizing about lunch. You may misunderstand the instructions you received and treat thoughts like they are the enemy. It's okay. This is why it's called practice. We practice being present with ourselves, fully and authentically. You are the only one who will ever really know your own mind. There is something empowering about learning how to develop and maintain a meditation practice on your own.

Whether you want the support of group practice, or feel ready to establish your own self-directed home practice, it helps to have some guidance. If you are just starting to meditate, see the Resources section for an introduction to the practice.

Perseverance

You know the drill: you have a goal, set an intention to get there, and a truckload of obstacles blocks your path. Like Naropa's relentless tests under Tilopa's guidance, perseverance can seem superhuman in the face of never-ending holdups.

Getting stuck is a part of the path—it's a part of life. Losing your perseverance happens when you lose sight of this fact—you assume staying stuck is a permanent situation. Feeling stuck shows up in a variety of ways: as an obstacle, a limited mindset. Or circumstances: the wrong place. The wrong time. Wrong people. Or you simply lose your mojo.

These self-made obstacles manifest differently for everyone. But what they have in common is fear. Fear is the obstacle. Because even if we can "blame" our circumstances or a seemingly irreversible twist of fate, if we hit a roadblock, it's fear calling us out.

Fear is the opposite of love.

Why do we let fear get in the way of our happiness? How do we persevere in the face of it? By showing up.

That's what perseverance is: showing up. Again and again. Even when you've long since let go of hope. Once you give up hope of attainment, that's when you have a chance to arrive. But here's the tricky part; you can't fake giving up hope in hopes of attaining something. It doesn't work that way. You have to actually let go of hope. And then show up anyway.

Hopelessness is not always a bad thing. This is why practice is so helpful; it mirrors perfectly the letting go of hope. Because what on earth are we hoping to attain through practice? It's so intangible. Much easier to simply stop altogether. But just when you start to wonder whether getting on your mat or your meditation cushion every day is really worth the effort, this is when things start to get interesting. When you commit to being present, set an intention, and simply show up, things start to change.

Daily Meditation Practice

When focusing on developing a daily meditation habit, start with short sessions. It's easier to develop confidence when you don't ask too much of yourself at first. I like to break up very short sessions— say ten minutes—with brief passages from meditation guidebooks. Then I sit with the instruction fresh in my mind while I try to put it into practice. Thrangu Rinpoche's commentary on *Pointing Out the Dharmakaya* is one of my favorites.

Here are a few tricks I've learned to develop and maintain a meditation or yoga practice:

1. **Schedule it.** Write an outline of practice for each day and display the schedule somewhere you cannot avoid seeing it. Something written on a schedule takes on a bit more importance and the mind tends to remember to do it. Even if you miss a session, or a day, if it is noted as a regular feature of your daily schedule, chances are you'll pay more attention to it.

2. **Identify support.** It's so helpful to have someone to talk to about meditation practice. It's even more helpful to have someone to do it with. If possible, find a "practice buddy" and sit together on a regular basis. Or if you live far apart, commit to a certain schedule and check in with each other to hold each other accountable. Talk with a guide who can steer you right when you go off course, or better yet, find a teacher you can study with. Attend a regular group practice session to keep in touch with your community.

3. **Keep learning.** Read books, attend programs with authentic teachers, participate in retreats.

Developing a meditation practice is never-ending. Unless you are Shakyamuni (the historical) Buddha, there is always another layer of subtlety to discover. Maintaining a meditation practice means doing the practice, whether or not you see signs of progress. Practice evolves despite our egoic commentary about that evolution. Just keep going. Study helps you refine your technique and your awareness. Practice and study are equally important.

4. **Forgive lapses.** Things happen. Sometimes you can't make it to the cushion, and well, as they say in Bhutan, "What to do?" The only way to move beyond a situation is to accept where you are. If you fight, you'll only prolong your misery, and the whole point of the meditation practice is to develop a sane and friendly relationship with your mind in order to transcend suffering. Let go and allow the process to unfold. Let go of attachment to how your practice looks, how it feels, or what others say about it. It doesn't matter. The practice is like a microscope for you to observe your experience. Whatever happens, it's no big deal.

Learning to develop and maintain a meditation practice is a lifelong journey. From this perspective, there is no end goal. Ego doesn't like that situation very much. Ego wants progress and signs of success. But if you train the mind to be present at all stages of the journey, your whole life becomes a pilgrimage. The way to start integrating this awareness into your life is to simply get on your cushion each day and watch what arises, without judgment. That's called the path of meditation.

Writing Practice: Your Daily Practice

Use the following prompts as starting-off points:

- What would it look like for you to establish a daily practice?
- Write down creative ways you can fit a daily practice into your schedule.
- How can you commit to making your daily practice a priority?
- Think about how you can get your family and friends to support your commitment to this practice.
- How will you respond if they push back at your plan?
- Create your own daily practice schedule—make it doable and appealing so that it's something you'll want to focus on every day.
- Identify the components of your practice—what practice will you do?
- When will you practice? Will you sit first thing in the morning and then practice some yoga asana? Will you start with early-morning yoga practice, and end in a long meditation? Will you alternate days? Will you meditate before bed?
- Where will you practice? Do you have a designated practice space in your home? Could you?
- Will you set up a shrine or altar? Will you sit on a cushion or a chair?

Get detailed about how your daily practice will manifest each day. Your daily practice forms the building blocks of your pilgrimage. Set yourself up for success on a daily basis and your journey will unfold on a strong foundation.

6

Navigating the Path

Surrender

Committing to a spiritual path involves surrendering our ego. A student asked me once what it means to surrender. She said, "I don't know what I am surrendering to."

When you surrender to the practice, it's not really surrendering to anything. It's just surrender: releasing the grip of constantly trying to better your own situation. You let go of your own agenda and open yourself to what naturally wants to arise.

Surrender is understanding that when you let go, you are not losing anything. What you surrender is the constant effort of trying to hold it together, which (correct me if I'm wrong) wasn't really working out anyway. Was it?

So you can surrender cheerfully. This involves a huge amount of trust, which develops through practice. The more you practice, the more you understand that you are not who you think you are. So to continue to invest time and energy boosting this nonexistent (and frankly demanding) ego loses its appeal.

It's important to let go of any results (or lack thereof) you might experience from practice. Ego is so invested in its own survival that it will take on anything as a badge of honor—including spiritual attainments. So if you notice yourself feeling discouraged or proud of your practice, let it go.

As Chögyam Trungpa Rinpoche noted, "If spirituality becomes a way of building ourselves up, then of course the whole process of surrendering is completely distorted."

So when you surrender any illusions of how your journey will look, and give up trying to attain something, you suddenly free up all that energy that would have otherwise been spent striving for unsustainable goals.

Perspective

Once upon a time I taught yoga in central Hong Kong, managing the studio at the Landmark Mandarin Oriental Hotel. It was an intense phase, living in the big, bustling, money-worshipping city. I had a hard time relaxing into the pace of that life.

Mandarin Oriental had strict guidelines. Their five-star requirements often drove me mad. My task was to maintain the integrity of teaching a spiritual tradition, while fulfilling the standardized needs of a luxury hotel corporation. They wanted me to create marketing plans, design corporate protocol trainings, fill out incident reports, and attend staff meetings. Our interests were incompatible. Their primary interest was the bottom line; mine was teaching people to breathe.

Maintaining this balance took its toll on my health. Insomnia became a regular feature of my night-life. I felt weak and tired, and every day someone told me I looked exhausted—because I was. The pollution levels in the city were off the charts. My strenuous asana practice drained me further. I felt like a phony to be teaching a discipline that didn't seem to bring me health and happiness anymore. With years of study and practice behind me, I suddenly didn't feel any happier or wiser. How could I have come all this way with yoga and feel so stressed out? I couldn't understand why—after so many years of disciplined spiritual practice and healthy living—I looked and felt so wretched. How could I stand up there in front of a class and pretend to know something about a peaceful state of mind? My mind was complete chaos.

I craved guidance and support. I needed hugs and someone to bring me a cup of tea when I got home. I hired a housekeeper to come once a week just to have the sensation that someone was looking after me. Sometimes I took a taxi home from work to let someone else drive for ten minutes. I went to Happy Foot Reflexology three times a week to sit in an oversize chair and have my feet rubbed for an hour while they brought me cup after cup of jasmine tea.

As a teacher, I felt obligated to be some sort of role model. Part of me loved this role. I loved watching students grow and blossom; I cherished the close relationships and confidences they shared. But role models, as far as I was concerned, did not fall apart. And this was precisely what I was doing: I was falling apart at the seams.

I started noticing that if I practiced Ashtanga too intensively, my nervous system would not settle in for a deep meditation. Since this was what I craved—the deep restful calm that arises with stable meditation—I realized I needed to seriously rethink my practice.

Standards and Diminishing Returns

Meanwhile, the Ashtanga system was evolving. Because of the booming popularity of Ashtanga, new students were flocking to Mysore. As a result, the practice was becoming more systematized. There were simply too many people to give individualized instruction, so guidelines helped to maintain standards for the masses.

Whereas Richard Freeman had originally taught me slow and precise awareness of the inner workings of the body during the yoga practice, Sharath insisted on having me take my toe (in trikonasana), or grab my thighs (in back-bending), which seemed to sabotage the alignment—and short circuit the flow of prana. The focus was on the achievement of an external result, rather than observing the flow of the energetic body. The difference was stark, and the "new" approach (new to me, anyway) did not resonate with me. It felt more like performance than practice.

New rules coming out of Mysore dictated how I had to teach if I wanted to maintain my authorization status. Guruji and Sharath insisted on biannual visits to Mysore with hefty fees, which was nearly impossible while holding down a six-day-a-week corporate job. I felt an increasingly narrow and rigid interpretation of how I could teach the Ashtanga practice.

I invited Richard to come teach in Hong Kong and I assisted him during the workshop. One evening we had dinner in a café in Kowloon overlooking Victoria Bay, the vague outline of Hong Kong's skyline obscured by a cold fog. The Star Ferryboats chugged through the dimming light, depositing commuters at the pier just in front of the café's terrace, neon blinking on as the daylight faded.

"I'm totally disillusioned with the evolution of Ashtanga," I told him, "and yet I'm so immersed in the system I don't know what else to do. Suddenly Ashtanga yoga feels so restricting. Not only the practice itself, but the whole culture that has developed around it. The politics. The rules. Maybe I should just shut up and join the crowd but I've never been a crowd follower."

Richard said, "You have to learn how to be in the system without being in the system."

But why would I want to be part of a system that imposes rules rather than encouraging me to listen to my inner wisdom?

Divorcing the System

Richard's workshop in Hong Kong marked a turning point. Though he was a direct student of K. Pattabhi Jois, Richard developed his own unique style of teaching. He taught guided classes, often using metaphor and humor to convey insights while students held postures, so a direct experience would arise.

In addition to the fact that he spoke English fluently—which K. Pattabhi Jois did not—he had an understanding of Western values and mind-set that helped plant Ashtanga Vinyasa Yoga in a new cultural context. So in a way he helped translate K. Pattabhi Jois's teachings. Because the traditional practice was done "Mysore style" in silence, with students doing their own practice at their own pace, there was rarely an opportunity in K. Pattabhi Jois's Ashtanga system to discuss things or convey deeper insights verbally as a teacher. So with new dictates coming out of Ashtanga HQ, I felt frustrated that I was unable to share tools to access deeper aspects of the practice. I was caught between the old school and the new school.

The pace in Hong Kong was unbearable. There was entirely too much happening. Suits, sirens, neon, typhoons, Lamborghinis, clusterfucks of umbrellas. I was sick and tired of all the cheap plastic crap, the new unnecessary electronics and the bright cutesy cartoons advertising them. I couldn't bear to see another happy loving couple, giggling over ice cream cones. Everything on God's green earth was available to buy or grasp for a moment of entertainment and I was just plain overwhelmed with it all. I was not interested in keeping up with the Joneses or the Chans. I was tired of speeding double-deckers and queues at the crosswalks, designer handbags and bubble tea; pigs roasting in the window-fronts while trim Armani-clad men scurried around at the lunch hour. Tired of dealing with a colleague who had developed a habit of sleeping with our students. The only things I wanted to see were snowy mountains, pine needles, and a bright blue expanse of sky.

I broke. One day after class, eating my lunch on a park bench overlooking the harbor, I reached my limit. I sat there sobbing into my salad as I realized I could take no more.

A few days later, early one morning (in my old life we called this late-night) before heading to the studio, I sat down to meditate as I did every day, and suddenly, something clicked. As I contemplated another full day with another sleepless night behind me, I settled for a moment into the deepest feeling of peace (or was that utter exhaustion?) I had ever known. A warm, cozy light illuminated me from inside as a wave of absolute contentment settled over me. I could have stayed there all day. A fire had been kindled in my belly and continued to glow warm orange embers. I buzzed with bliss like a dizzy love glow. I didn't want to get up. I craved more time on the cushion stoking that fire. It was like I had fallen in love with meditation. That was what I wanted to cultivate and share with people.

Once, in Mysore, I had asked Guruji about meditation. I wanted to know the view of meditation according to the Ashtanga system.

He laughed.

"You practice," he said. That was it.

There was no formal instruction for working with the mind in the Ashtanga system—no clear guidance for the meditation practice. Suddenly I realized that Ashtanga Vinyasa Yoga was proving to be an incomplete spiritual path for me. I needed teachings to help guide me in working with my mind, to give me some context for the whole practice.

When approached with awareness and sensitivity—as I had learned it from Richard—the Ashtanga practice is brilliant. But the evolving rules and regulations had distorted that system into something unrecognizable. The strict guidelines that prohibited authorized teachers from traveling to teach, or from teaching the intermediate series—even though this is the series that most of us were practicing—didn't make sense to me. Guruji insisted that the practice be presented in a formulaic system, with no room for deviation.

Seriously? I've got the wisdom of the goddess inside me, and access to her wisdom, and I'm "not allowed" to teach anything apart from the set sequence of physical postures of Ashtanga Vinyasa Yoga? It felt like asking an artist to teach paint by numbers. Or like handing me the keys to a Ferrari that I can only drive in the parking lot. Rather than encouraging students to become authentic teachers themselves, to find their own way, it felt like we were being monitored by the religious police.

My intuition told me that spirituality was not about jumping through hoops or adhering to rules. This regimentation inhibited the freshness of the practice. And I was no longer interested in following someone else's rules.

My teaching authorization was about to expire, and I needed to decide whether or not to renew it. I loved Guruji and Sharath, but I could not pretend to adhere to a set of rules that no longer reflected my truth. Teaching with integrity was more important to me than a certificate I could paste on my wall—and that would expire if I didn't return regularly to pay outrageous fees to practice with a groping guru.

I was done.

Groping Gurus

For the sake of transparency, I will say that while nothing untoward transpired on my first trip, on later visits to Mysore I did experience K. Pattabhi Jois's infamous groping. Sometimes it was innocuous, and sometimes it was blatant and gratuitous. Hand on crotch, hand on ass, crotch to crotch, while pulling me backward in a variation of downward dog. It didn't help me deepen into the posture, so I can't say it was done with an intent to assist.

I never did speak up about this, except in private conversations with my Ashtanga girlfriends. I don't know why I didn't speak up. Part of it was that it felt more bizarre and incongruous than predatory. Part of it was that while I was practicing (and this is when the groping occurred—when he came to adjust me) I was so engrossed in the intensity of the posture, it was as if my mind couldn't hold both thoughts at once. So the experience quickly left my radar as I returned my attention to the intense posture I was doing.

I have a hard time condemning a dead man whose practice saved my life. I have sweet memories of him assisting me (benignly) with postures, chatting, and hosting us for meals at his home. Huge groups of us were invited, his staff and family serving us while we sat on the floor of his home eating off of banana leaves—exquisite meals and gracious receptions. His students clearly mattered to him, and I have no doubt that his intention was to help us grow beyond our limited beliefs. I cannot forget that and go on the offense against him for something that I don't understand, and perhaps he didn't either.

Perhaps I was simply in denial after having experienced so much of this type of unwanted sexual attention throughout my life. I just took it to be part of a woman's life. Thank goodness that's now changing. The point is to be present with what's happening and speak your truth in the moment—and I am guilty of not doing this. I did not speak up in the moment. Live and learn. That's why we practice.

Richard had a way of describing correct conduct in the yoga teaching situation: "don't splatter your bindu." Bindu has a variety of complex meanings, but could be loosely translated as your life force seed—it also means "drop" or "semen." So Richard's pithy instruction on avoiding sexual misconduct means that beyond acting and speaking with pure intention, you keep your mind clean while interacting with students. Since mind creates energetic waves, students feel when something is "off." So to teach with integrity (as Richard always did in my experience) you have to monitor your body, speech, and mind. Which, coincidentally, is the practice of yoga.

If you find yourself in a sangha whose leadership you question, you have to take responsibility for yourself. Once you've said your piece, your truth, you decide on the correct action to take, which in my case was leaving the lineage. Then you either carry on or move on and let it go.

Those are two distinct steps, so just to reiterate:

1. Carry on or move on.
2. Let go.

Courage

There's a big difference between commitment to practice and attachment to the circumstances the practice is clothed in. When it is no longer about listening to your own experience, but rather about trying to adhere to a set of rules reflecting someone else's experience, practice can get stale.

It takes courage to disentangle yourself from the clan when that happens. Straying from the pack can be lonely and confusing. But breakthroughs rarely occur by following someone else's rules.

Does the fact that I refuse to play the administrative game of keeping my authorization up to date undermine my ability to teach? Does it erase the years of intensely dedicated practice behind me? Does it affect the commitment I've made to my own practice?

I'd been hesitant to fess up, for fear of alienating people in the Ashtanga community, but more truthfully, I was afraid of being judged as a quitter. The truth is that I have not quit, I have simply expanded my repertoire to include other practices and learned to adapt. Injury, age, and a need for a more expansive view urged me to find other ways to practice. I couldn't reconcile how expanding the mind could be achieved by limiting myself to one particular point of view.

My departure from the Ashtanga teachers circle does not necessarily have to reflect badly on the lineage, or the teachers of the tradition. Ashtanga changed my life for the better—the practice is brilliant. It was certainly a necessary stepping stone on my path. But once you step on a stone to get to the other side, do you really have to pick up that stone and put it in your backpack? You can simply turn around, bow to the stone in reverence and gratitude for having facilitated your passage, and then go on your merry way.

Shakyamuni Buddha gave up his credentials when he left his palace. Perhaps, like him, you feel a need to make your own way, despite resistance from an established tradition. You can give up the affiliation without giving up the inquiry.

The Buddha's example offers a whole set of practices each appropriate to certain periods, phases, and aspects of life. (A great book to learn about the Buddha's life story is *Old Path White Clouds* by Thich Nhat Hanh.) There is no "one size fits all" spiritual practice. The Dalai Lama admits that if a practice is not bringing about beneficial results, then we should question whether that practice is the right one for us in the circumstances.

> When we take medicine, it is not the taste, color, or quantity of the medicine that matters; the important thing is the beneficial effect on our body. If in spite of having taken a certain medicine for a long time we see no effect, there is no point in continuing to take it. Regardless of

whether your practice is elaborate or short, above all,
it should be effective in bringing about some kind of a
transformation, a change for the better, within you.
                    —His Holiness the Dalai Lama

The main point is to develop a connection to a true wisdom
practice that allows genuine inquiry into the big questions about
life. My allegiance is not to any particular system, but to the
ongoing practice of self-inquiry. I don't mean to advocate a
shopping spree in the spiritual market—you have to stick with
something to get to the heart of things. But commitment is
different from attachment.

What is the difference? I would say it comes down to ego. If you
hold too tightly to anything—or take it too seriously—you should
be suspicious. I find that often the people who seem to have the
deepest insights are the ones with the best—and most irreverent—
sense of humor. Ultimate truths are not affected by the categories
you create. Awareness of these truths is not exclusive to any
particular system. Fundamentalism about anything will keep you
stuck. The correct practice is the one that is most appropriate for you.

Practice is a tool, a guide rope leading you through a dark
cave so you can make your way to the light. But when a bit of
daylight comes, you've had some insight, and the rope is no longer
necessary. You have to trust the inner guide at some point and take
responsibility for yourself. Ultimately, it is up to you.[8]

But this leaves plenty of room for interpretation. Some say it
is good to eat meat if you have a certain blood type; others say
eating meat is cruel and the primary cause of global warming that
harms us all. Some say that all yoga teachers should be authorized
through a system of standardized procedures; others say adherence
to systemic dissemination of yoga philosophy inhibits or even

prevents true yogic awareness from developing. Some advocate secret relationships as a path to spiritual awakening; some think this is bullshit and a creepy excuse for certain teachers to abuse positions of power while distorting the spirit of the teachings. Certain traditions say following a lineage or a guru is essential to success in spiritual practice; and sometimes charlatans present themselves as wisdom masters and lure students into deception. Some say lineage is necessary, others notice that lineages are often broken by splitting in the sangha, creating devastating scars for its members.

This is not a new phenomenon. It is as old as the Buddha himself. When he realized that emaciating himself was not getting him any closer to nirvana, the Buddha chose to drink a bowl of milk offered by a well-intentioned girl who saw that he was starving. This benign act earned him the scorn of his five closest disciples, who were convinced that asceticism was the way to go. They publicly renounced him. In the modern world, that might look like giving back your yoga teacher certification.

So who do you believe? How do you find your way?

Perhaps the path comes down to this: a commitment to looking again and again at the present moment, to keep asking the hard questions, and an allegiance to uncovering what is true and good.

Formal practice is very useful as a tool to keep your intentions pure. But once a practice gets systematized, it necessarily develops a culture around it. Many spiritual practices and the format in which they are presented were intended for a vastly different audience in another era. Even if the practice was good for that particular culture, it doesn't necessarily mean it will be good for all cultures and at all times.

If you don't keep your discriminating awareness alive, blindly accepting everything that is served to you, you risk turning a valuable opportunity for spiritual inquiry into a ritual-based religion. And religion is at the root of most wars.

In the end, we come here alone; we leave here alone. No one else knows your inner journey as well as you do. So it is up to you to recognize what works and what doesn't. Do you have the courage to give up attachment to a preordained path and commit to asking an open question? At a certain point, the biggest step you can take on the path to awakening is to trust yourself.

Even if that means swearing allegiance to a teacher.

Mind to Mind: Meeting the Teacher

There is a saying: when the student is ready, the teacher appears. Toward the end of my time in Hong Kong a friend wrote to let me know about a Bhutanese Buddhist teacher coming to give teachings. I called to inquire about the program, but it was full. Dzongsar Khyentse Rinpoche would teach in Taipei the following weekend, so I booked a flight and a hotel for the weekend.

At the opening talk a Western man sat down next to me. We exchanged a few words in English—though he had a slight French accent—and settled in for the evening talk. I did not see him for the rest of the weekend.

Walking off the flight from Taipei back to Hong Kong Monday morning, I noticed a man staring at me—it was the French man who sat next to me at the teachings. We had ended up on the same flight. When we recognized each other, we both smiled at the coincidence and chatted on the way to passport control.

He had been personal assistant to a Tibetan Buddhist lama for several years. He offered to introduce me to him.

The following week, Fabrice showed up at Starbucks as promised. He took me by bus to Kennedy Town and ushered me into his teacher's private quarters. I sat on a couch waiting to be called. When the door opened suddenly, Rinpoche looked up, our eyes met, and he flashed a smile bright as lightning: blinding, sudden, direct. Blood rushed to my head and I took a deep breath to keep the tears from welling over. I loved him immediately.

Rinpoche invited me in.

He was enormous, filling the room entirely with his presence. I entered, offered three half prostrations and a kata, the traditional white scarf, then I sat down to speak with him. I had an overwhelming urge to poke him to see if he was actually there in front of me. It was like he did not really exist. Though he was massive—he must have weighed over 250 pounds—he was diaphanous, and I couldn't tell if he was really there or a sort of holograph. Whatever was there was good, and I felt like a planet magnetized by this being. We spoke for several minutes. I am not exactly sure what happened there, but something did.

Cosmic Redirect

Fabrice and I developed an easy friendship. My infrequent meetings with him uplifted my spirits, but I was still exhausted from the life I was living in Hong Kong. I wanted to go on retreat. I had already asked Mandarin Oriental for a six-week leave of absence. I should have gone to Mysore to renew my teaching authorization, but the last thing I needed was more crowds of yoga students and 4:00 a.m. wake-up calls. What I needed was to sit in meditation, reflect and recharge my batteries.

I booked a flight to Koh Samui, in Thailand. At the farthest end of the island I found a quiet hut on the beach surrounding a calm cove. I settled into a slow rhythm of practice, writing, reading, and swimming. I reveled in the simple pleasure of being able to sleep again.

I practiced morning and evening, a set program of various meditation techniques involving visualizations and chanting, and gentle yoga. I discovered that when I maintained a softer, gentler asana practice my meditation became more settled. I studied a couple of Buddhist texts I had brought with me. I ate simply, mostly fruit and cereal, and once in a while I borrowed a scooter to get takeout curry from an organic restaurant nearby. In the evenings I walked ten steps to sit on the beach and listen to the wind and waves.

In the yoga world, people often spoke about retreat as if it were synonymous with "holiday." My understanding of the word came from my first retreat as part of my Naropa University program when we practiced meditation ten hours a day, no speaking, no reading, no music or communication.

My first solitary retreat was a hugely powerful experience and something I wanted more of. There is a level of settledness that is impossible (for me) to experience in the company of others, with the always-present possibility of communication. Group retreats are also powerful in their own way, but solo practice had become a staple of my spiritual diet, and it had been too long since I'd been nourished that way. Even though I often felt so alone in Hong Kong, it was always that "lonely in a crowd" feeling. Being truly alone was such a different, powerful experience. That kind of alone was nothing like loneliness; that kind of alone fed me.

I had no desire to return to work and play the game anymore. Hong Kong was like 99 percent dark chocolate…looks so good and rich and you get all excited for that first bite, but you just can't take it. You wonder whether you can just spit it out without anyone noticing. You need something a bit sweeter. There were a lot of material perks—my spacious downtown apartment, the stellar salary, the convenient location so I could travel around Asia for holidays and the money to do it. I gave it my best shot, but it was not a situation I could maintain. What I really wanted to do was practice meditation.

Back in Hong Kong I submitted my resignation. I stopped doing a full intermediate or advanced ashtanga practice. I went to Nepal and sat for three months at a monastery above Kathmandu. I resumed prostrations—the first of the foundational practices of Vajrayana Buddhism.

What might appear as a dead end or deviation on the path often points to a radically new way of being. But there is a moment before you leap when you don't actually know if it's the right thing to do. You have to let go to find out.

Writing Practice: Navigation Tools

Do a free write for each of the following prompts:

- What signs have you been ignoring?
- What or who do you need to limit your exposure to?
- What old patterns or circumstances no longer serve you?
- What influence leads you astray?
- What do you still do that you know is harmful for you?
- Who leaves you feeling drained or unappreciated?
- What positive changes have you already made?
- What do you long to invite into your experience?

7

Developing Confidence

Retreat

One of the most powerful aspects of going on pilgrimage is retreating from busyness—the daily responsibilities and schedule that normally make up your life. These regular features not only define the quality of your life, but also outline your identity.

When you extract yourself from your habitual environment, you invite the possibility of a new identity to emerge. This can mean going into long retreat in an isolated cabin, or a cave. Maybe it means a motorcycle journey over the Tibetan plateau, or a walk through the Spanish countryside. I once rented a bungalow near the beach on a remote Vietnamese island, for seven months. It was a fantastic retreat—no one to talk to (language barriers and no Internet), plenty of fresh fruit, and a big isolated room to practice all day. Lizard entertainment. Late-afternoon swimming meditation on the deserted beach. Once you have the internal structure in place—your practice instructions and some discipline—you can go anywhere.

You might protest: what if I can't take time out for a retreat? Perhaps you must go to work every day or take care of your family—you can still establish a retreat-like environment by setting boundaries. I know people who have created a semblance of retreat even in the midst of their daily lives. You can include your "worldly" activities as part of your retreat practice—this has the added benefit of helping you bring the fruits of your meditation into your daily life. You could eliminate social events and extraneous conversations for a period of time and spend that time on your meditation cushion. Maybe you don't have the luxury of taking two weeks off, but could you sit when your children leave for school? Could you come straight home from work and head right into your meditation room?

What's important is to disconnect from the daily distractions and let your mind settle. It's hard to get into deeper states of meditation when you are constantly poised to respond to external prompts: the phone, e-mail, newspapers, neighbors, text messages. It may be hard at first, but you can train people not to expect you to reply immediately. It really comes down to your own self-discipline and willingness to let go.

Unplugging

Twenty years ago when I opened a Hotmail account, I wrote my first e-mail from Mysore. Before that, there was a mail bin in the foyer of the shala, and we would wait two or three weeks for letters from home.

Back then it felt like magic to communicate in real time. Fast forward to today and we discover that too much connectivity has unfortunate side effects. This magical machinery that transformed our lives by creating constant connectivity has disconnected us from deeper parts of ourselves.

Many of us no longer sit quietly to watch a sunset, or sit in a sidewalk café simply to observe the flow of life, or open a hardback book to read—much less compose a handwritten letter. These are precious gifts, and habits I developed early in my life, my precursors to contemplative practice. I would hate to imagine life without them.

The Internet has robbed us of some of the serendipity that occurs with travel, and this is a key part of any pilgrimage. You don't know who you are going to meet along the way. You open yourself to whatever arises. These days, you wouldn't dream of getting on an airplane to India without having a hotel reservation, or without even knowing if the teacher you are going to study with is in town. (K. Pattabhi Jois wasn't, when I first arrived in 1997!) But in this case you close off many opportunities for chance encounters. When I called (on a landline) from Varanasi and learned K. Pattabhi Jois was not teaching at the moment, I decided to travel to Mysore and wait for him. He showed up a few days after I arrived, and as a result I was able to study with him in a very intimate setting—there were twelve of us practicing with him. Sometimes when you trust your instincts—rather than information—you get extraordinary gifts.

Setting boundaries allows the space necessary for transformation to occur. You wouldn't expect a new relationship to thrive without setting aside some private time. Relationships need nourishment and privacy to delve deep into things. This is also true for your practice—you are developing a relationship with your inner wisdom.

You might need to give yourself permission to step outside your daily life to seek deeper truths. Of course you need to take care of your responsibilities. But isn't it your duty to live out your full potential? Isn't it your responsibility to be happy? Try disconnecting from the daily distractions on a regular basis, even if it's for a set amount of time each day. This one simple habit will have profound effects.

Fair warning: you will most likely not get this permission from people in your current circles. People get nervous when someone steps outside of the box—there is a strong tendency to try to pull her back in, like a potful of crabs about to boil. "If we are going to boil alive, then so are you, my friend."

So permission will have to come from you.

When you change your daily habits without awareness—you start eating more cake, having that extra glass of wine in the evening, or start the morning with e-mail instead of a walk or a yoga practice or picking up your pen or paintbrush—then the tone of your day is set. Combine a string of days, and the tone of your life is set.

And the opposite is true: small conscious changes over time can have profound effects on your state of mind.

Yoga and Meditation Practice

You are extremely fortunate to live in a time when esoteric spiritual practices are readily available. But you need to be a bit savvy if you want to really benefit from the practices.

Yoga prepares the system for meditation. Ashtanga yoga, in particular, is a systematized path to meditation. Traditionally, sitting meditation is not taught in the Ashtanga system. The logic goes like this: once the body is prepared and purified, meditation will happen on its own. I like to believe this. I also think it helps to encourage it; to develop it through formal practice. I see it as a way of expanding the dimensions of the yoga practice.

The eight limbs of yoga—Yama, Niyama, Asana, Pranayama, Pratyahara, Dharana, Dhyana, and Samadhi—are your map.

Essentially, the entire path of yoga is a meditation practice. But if you look at all the yoga classes happening in studios around the world these days, you might not immediately see this connection. You might have to find a separate teacher or center to get proper instruction on meditation practice. The two approaches to practice—yoga asana and meditation—are definitely compatible, and if you undertake both, you'll have rocket fuel under your asana.

Simplicity

You know that sense of ease when you watch a professional athlete doing their thing? They make it look so easy. Simplicity is the hallmark of a pro.

Keep it simple. Come back to the practice you are doing. When you notice yourself making stories, thinking thoughts about things, acknowledge that, and come back. Back to awareness of breath, body, movement, stillness, mind. Find the stillness within movement.

When you are learning a new practice or posture, it is important to stick to the traditional instructions. Later, when you have some experience, you can improvise a bit. But like a good musician, technique is required before you have the skill to play your heart out.

Thinking is ego's domain; thoughts to reinforce your version of yourself and the world. So the point of practice is NOT about thinking, but coming back to experience: of breath, of movement or stillness and awareness. Breath provides a focus; movement and stillness provide a context. Coming back to the breath again and again interrupts the mental stream—it cuts the never-ending chatter that occupies our mind in the usual daily context. You override that by coming back to the awareness of breath. This is an important point, because it is possible to go through years of breathing practice thinking that you are practicing awareness of breath, without actually practicing awareness of breath. There is a big difference!

Be aware of your breath. Try it now. As you breathe in, notice that you are breathing in. As you breathe out, notice that you are breathing out.

I love this simple practice from the great Vietnamese Buddhist Master Thich Nhat Hanh:

> Breathing in, I know I am breathing in.
> Breathing out, I know I am breathing out.

Breathing in, I notice my in-breath has become deeper.
Breathing out, I notice that my out-breath has become
    slower . . .
Breathing in, I calm myself.
Breathing out, I feel at ease.
Breathing in, I smile.
Breathing out, I release.
Breathing in, I dwell in the present moment.
Breathing out, I feel it is a wonderful moment.

Applied Mindfulness

If you have ever tried to follow the breath in meditation, you know that the mind wanders easily away from the present moment—it has a tendency to get distracted. When your distracted mind is left unchecked for prolonged periods, you may end up ignoring entire aspects of your life.

When you are able to focus the mind for a while, you start to recognize your habitual patterns. Not all habitual patterns are bad—washing your hands after changing the kitty litter is probably a good one to keep. Maxing out your credit card on a retail therapy binge whenever you have a bad day at work might become problematic. Once you are able to see the patterns, then you can start to ask yourself: Do I really want to keep doing this?

Luckily, you have a choice. You recognize this choice by practicing mindfulness. Start simply by sitting down to watch your mind in meditation. If you do this on a regular basis, and maintain a certain degree of focus and discipline, you will—sooner or later—start to experience moments of clarity and presence.

How do you do this?

Make a habit of checking in with your breath. Notice your breath when you are on the computer, or talking to a friend, or driving to an appointment. Get to know how the breath changes with your state of mind. From a yogic perspective, when the "winds"[9] are disturbed, the mind will be agitated. When you settle the breath into a rhythmic flow, the mind also settles. Whenever you notice you are distracted, return again to the experience of breath entering and leaving the body. This is a first step toward settling the mind.

Confidence comes from developing this experience. When you can rely on yourself to stay present through thick and thin, you can handle just about anything.

Settling the Mind

Think of a jar filled with water and sand. When it is shaken, the sand swirls around, clouding the water. This is what a distracted mind is like—no clarity. A settled state of mind is characterized by clarity.

The most direct way to achieve this settled state of mind is through the practice of sitting meditation. When you have practiced this for a while you develop the capacity to bring this calm clarity to your daily life.

Recognize thoughts as impermanent and insubstantial. After all, where are they? Can you grab one?

When you ally with the spaciousness of the mind instead of the contents of the mind (thoughts and emotions) you automatically shift your perspective. This allows you to more fully focus on whatever you choose.

But, while mindfulness may provide temporary relief of ignorance—the tendency to avoid the truth of what is right in front of us—it won't alleviate emotional suffering over the long term.

In order to witness your destructive patterns—the habits of body, speech, and mind that cause you to suffer—you need to take a step back and develop a wider perspective. For that you need awareness, which arises through expanding your view. So the key to making mindfulness applicable to daily life is to develop awareness.

Awareness

Mindfulness is bringing your focus back to the task at hand, whether you are observing the breath in meditation or chopping carrots. Awareness is remembering to be mindful of what you are doing. So when you get distracted during meditation, or suddenly the soup boils over on the stove, you come back and remember your focus. You attend to the distraction, return to the breath, or to the carrots, and resume your mindfulness—tending to whatever you have chosen as your object of attention.

The only way to interrupt bad habits that cause suffering is to first become aware of them. In practicing mindfulness and awareness, you learn about your own tendencies and idiosyncrasies. Once you are able to see your patterns, you can apply antidotes necessary to bring yourself back into balance.

If I have a tendency to get defensive when provoked, I can learn to stay physically present and engaged. If I easily fly into a rage, I can learn to slow down my reactivity by remembering a mindfulness technique. If I have a tendency to be lazy, I can learn to create structures that motivate me.

Awareness is the great medicine that allows you to heal your emotional wounds. Without your imbalances—your heartbreaks, struggles, disappointments and obstacles—there would be no journey to take—no need to seek medicine. So you should also bow to your weaknesses, in gratitude. They are the gatekeepers.

Your greatest obstacle is your greatest strength.

Awareness leads to recognition of the interconnected nature of every aspect of our experience. You start to see how relaxing the body and deepening the breath affects your state of mind. Eventually you start to see how every thought, word, and action sends out waves that affect the subtle details of your environment and relationships.

The dawning of awareness arises when you are able to sustain relaxed mindfulness of the present moment. It happens naturally when you are fully present, engaged, and relaxed. Say you are in conversation over dinner with your beloved, and he or she is telling you all the reasons you are so wonderful. You would probably be so riveted by these words that you would not be at all distracted by the child screaming in the restaurant, or the clatter of plates as the waiters rush about, or by the little spinach leaf on his tooth. Mindfulness is what keeps your ears tuned in to the words; awareness is recognizing what is happening in the present situation—the context. Essentially, there is no effort involved in awareness. The practice is to stay focused and relaxed in equal measures.

Awareness is observing the process of being mindful; it is conscious involvement in whatever we are doing. If mindfulness is continuously coming back to the present moment, awareness is recognizing the context in which mindfulness takes place. Mindfulness + awareness = presence.

How do you bring mindfulness and awareness to your pilgrimage?

Presence

Being fully present is surprisingly challenging. It's so easy to opt out of the present in favor of a juicy fantasy. If you are waiting for a certain outcome, you may miss signs that don't align with your expectations. Presence is essentially being fully embodied, here, now, without imposing our expectations.

This is a great practice to do while on a journey. One of my favorite practices while traveling in a foreign country—or to a new part of my country—is to simply observe without trying to decipher anything. Allow the sights, sounds, smells—the feel of the heat, the taste of new food—to simply wash over you without having to identify or categorize it. Try to suspend judgment long enough to have a direct experience. Sometimes I take myself out on "artist dates" (if you don't know about these see Julia Cameron's *The Artist's Way*) and just watch the world as if viewing a great art exhibit.

A traditional analogy is of a child in a Tibetan temple—experiencing the dazzling sights, sounds, smells—the whole atmosphere will leave an impression. But the child has no idea what any of it means. The significance of the images, the words being spoken, the rituals—everything will be meaningless. But the experience will leave an imprint, a mood.

While you are observing your surroundings, imagine you are like a child who is seeing things for the first time. Don't assume you know what's going on. Make note of the details of your environment. Tune in to your body to see what messages it is picking up. Notice the body language and facial expressions of others. Listen with your inner ear, or your sixth sense. Open your mind to possibilities you have not yet imagined. Just as there is a difference between hearing and listening with the ears, let the mind "listen."

Presence Enables You to Weather Storms with Greater Ease

It's easy to engage in destructive patterns when you're not aware of them. You get overwhelmed and go into "reaction mode." There is a stimulus—like someone saying something hurtful—that sparks a feeling. You don't like it, you don't want to feel it, and so you hurry to find an escape from that feeling. You lash out, run away, pick up a cigarette, quit the job, ditch the partner—anything to distract you from the physical sensations of a disturbing emotion. When you slow the whole process down by using the practice of presence, you give yourself a pause to check in and choose an alternative response.

What does all of this have to do with your pilgrimage? Becoming aware of your own habits through mindfulness practice allows you the freedom to choose consciously to engage in behaviors and patterns, rather than being dragged along by a lifetime's worth of struggle. You can learn to ally with the spaciousness of the present moment instead of reacting to the content of the storyline. So this process of applying mindful awareness to your daily life offers the possibility of resting in a balanced state of mind no matter what the moment brings, so you remain open to whatever arises.

That's powerful medicine.

Guided Mindfulness Meditation

Look for the "Introduction to Sitting Meditation" in the Resources section on page 220.

Take the posture simply, with dignity and grace, but without hope or pride. We are not doing anything spectacular or particularly noteworthy. We are just sitting down, and for a period of time allowing ourselves to become aware of our experience of the present. It can be quite boring. If it is, then just notice that. If you have an ecstatic experience of bliss and suddenly see the light, then just notice that, and come back to the present in all its mundane detail. The idea is that, in the absolute sense, one state of mind is not preferable to another. Whether we have thoughts of divine inspiration or of what we will eat for breakfast, the response is the same: notice what happened, and then come back to earth, the breath, the body.

Writing Practice: Developing Confidence

Sit for ten minutes. Then use the following prompts and write for ten to twenty minutes on each one:

- What am I aware of right now?
- Where do I show up with full 100 percent presence?
- What are the signs that I am present?
- What gives me confidence?
- What disturbs my confidence?
- What is happening right now?

There is no right or wrong way to do this and it may feel simplistic. The point of this exercise is to help you tune in to a more refined awareness of your experience in the moment. Think of it as writing meditation practice.

8

Confusion

Adapting

Perhaps you've packed up your home, put your life on hold, and find yourself traveling in a remote part of the world with an open stretch of time ahead of you. Your pilgrimage is real.

What happens when you finally get to your dreamed-of destination, your sacred paradise, only to find that your niggling doubts, your habitual patterns, your fundamental discontent, have followed you here? The holy land you heard about is teeming with noisy tourists, the temple grounds littered with plastic. Hawkers assault you with overpriced, fake, or illegal goods and services. The tropical wildlife sends you screaming and scrambling onto the nearest piece of furniture, which breaks upon contact. You can't figure out how to find the travel agent because the streets don't have names and no one answers the phone (not that anyone there speaks English even if they did). Or when you finally do get there, the computers are down, or they are out to lunch. For the week.

The sooner you let go, the easier it will be.

How do you make the most of your time on pilgrimage when you are just not feeling it? How do you manage your mind when it is conspiring to bring you down just when you've decided to take some time to find inner peace?

Travel itself is one of the best practices I know. It forces you to come to terms with aspects of yourself you might not confront in your everyday life—things that come up when your environment is unknown, unexpected, changing, and often challenging. Or, to put it more directly, frustrating as hell.

In these situations, rather than fixating on—or scowling at—what's going on around you, look at your resistance. What are you unwilling to accept? When confronted with things that challenge your expectations or beliefs, you struggle to maintain your sense of identity. Look at your preconceived ideas to see where you might let go.

Humor helps.

It's easy to complain about inefficient systems and poorly functioning organizations. But if you had wanted the known, you would have stayed home, right? You asked for an adventure, so here it is. Adventure doesn't always come in the guise you expect or ask for.

Release expectations of how you thought your journey would unfold and let the path reveal itself, regardless of your preferences. Learn to be flexible in the face of sudden change or conflict.

Take a deep breath. Repeat.

When you can appreciate the similarities and differences, then travel becomes a joyful practice of observation. You start to see there are other ways of doing things. You can start to question if the way you learned to do things works for you. It gives you options to make changes or adjustments to your own life if you choose to.

Part of the education of travel is seeing how people from different cultures approach and manage life. But apart from seeing the differences, you start to see how utterly similar humans are, regardless of the culture that raised us. We all smile and laugh and experience emotions. We may behave differently and do different things with these emotions but the emotions themselves are universal. This one understanding can change the way you approach your life and make you more sensitive to and of those around you. It can open the door to compassion. Buddhists call this the seed of enlightenment.

Learning to adapt creates a strong mental health. Children naturally bounce back with resilience and just keep going with the flow—there is wisdom in this. There is a slogan from the lojong trainings of Mahayana Buddhism that goes like this:

In postmeditation, be a child of illusion.

In other words, don't assume things are solid and real or that you understand everything that's happening. Allow for things to unfold without knowing how or why. Watch the play of the phenomenal world with innocent eyes, as if in a dream. When you can rest in your center without depending on the stability of the outer world, you'll surprise yourself with an increased sense of confidence and well-being, knowing you can handle whatever challenge comes your way with strength and grace.

Pain versus Suffering

Inevitably along your journey, you will confront yourself. Your worst fear will raise its ugly head, or sorrow will push you in the mud. We humans are vulnerable. If you don't feel that way occasionally, you are probably in denial.

Pain is what happens when you don't get what you want, or you get what you don't want. Or you get what you want and then lose it. It happens to everyone, pretty much all of the time. It's not really a problem, unless you make it one.

Suffering is what happens when you see pain as a problem and try to avoid it. With practice, it's possible to learn to remain unattached to outcomes and accept the pain life dishes out. When you relate to your pain cleanly, without adding insult to injury, you may hurt in the moment, but then you let go. You learn to stay in the moment and move on from negative experiences more quickly instead of dragging your pain around with you. This is what it means to let go of the distractions that keep you from living our life's purpose of being fully in the present moment. You learn to, as a friend often says, "Keep Buggering On." KBO.

You can't really just tell yourself you won't struggle anymore—there is a whole lifetime of momentum behind that habitual pattern. But you can set an intention not to do so anymore. This is what practice means. You set an intention to be fully in the present moment, and then you learn tools to practice letting that happen more regularly.

Notice I say "letting" and not "making" that happen. You can't force presence. You just have to stop doing what's keeping you from being present, and get out of your own way.

Confronting Your Demons

Daily practice provides a sort of lab setting where you can observe your mental habits under a microscope. Once you've had a chance to look around a bit, you'll soon discover your demons. You'll recognize the emotions that hold you back or trigger you to react. You'll start to notice your resistance and your style of checking out. You might identify attachments and fears.

We all have ways of dealing with the stress of life, some more helpful and healthy than others. You get to know your habitual patterns by observing your mind. Admittedly, this can be painful and the process can look daunting at first.

Once in Phnom Penh I came across a fabulous boutique run by Italian designers. They help struggling Cambodian women make gorgeous handbags out of…trash. They recycle fishing nets and plastic bags and milk cartons to make whimsical and stylish accessories.

This is what you can do with your baggage. If you managed to combat an addiction, you are now an expert on recovery and your gift is that you can guide people to kick the habit. If you transformed your financial downfall into a spiritual awakening, you can help others who suffer the same predicament. Life WILL give you lemons occasionally. It's up to you whether you make fizzy lavender lemonade or squeeze them directly into your open wounds.

Obstacles

Obstacles: those pesky little details that block your way, prevent you from getting where you want to go, delaying your train just long enough to make you miss your next five connections. Just when you get your shit together professionally, your personal life falls apart. Or vice versa. Hated or feared beasts, obstacles make you doubt the quality of your practice and wonder what you have done to deserve such bitter frustration. Why can't things go right, just once?

The problem is not the obstacle. The problem is your thinking. Obstacles are not blocking your path: Obstacles ARE your path. Each bump in the road trains you to be a better driver.

Sometimes life throws up obstacles in the form of uncertainty. You don't know where to head next and the signs are unclear. Skillfully working with obstacles is a major part of establishing a solid foundation on a spiritual path, and an essential component of emotional well-being.

Once I had a client who doubted her ability to negotiate curves in her professional life. The stress of her job, plus the uncertainty of not knowing what came next caused her to suffer a variety of unpleasant symptoms. So I asked her a simple question. You could ask yourself this.

Do you really need to make this decision yet?

Some of us like to do what I call "preworrying." It's when you worry about a situation before there is anything you can do about it. It's a useless activity at best, a waste of time, and at its worst, can bring on a whole host of ailments, including anxiety, migraines, and panic attacks.

There is a quote I love by Shantideva from the classic *A Guide to the Bodhisattva Way of Life*:

"Why be unhappy about something if it can be remedied?
And what is the use of being unhappy about something if
it cannot be remedied?"

Obstacles are merely temporary blocks to where you think you are headed. Here is the clincher: they are often the good news you seek, guiding you somewhere you might not have even imagined. If you are open to change and pay attention to obstacles that arise in your life, you may be surprised by the serendipitous outcome.

The key to successfully working with obstacles is to relax. Make friends with the situation. Let go of your expectations and become curious about what new perspectives are coming into view. Be open to new possibilities and see where life takes you.

Pilgrimage is perfect for this type of practice. I can't tell you how many times I've missed planes, trains or taxis, only to have an opportunity that never would have occurred otherwise. It only looks like an obstacle if you are attached to the original outcome that you've made up in your mind.

Working with obstacles is a lifelong skill. Life doesn't always go your way. When you learn to relax into uncertainty, obstacles may appear not as difficulties or blocks, but rather as beacons on the horizon.

Working with particular obstacles—your particular obstacles—gives you experience that you can apply to other areas of your life. I learned at a certain point to be grateful for being single. It has allowed me a freedom and independence that few attached women have.

Your greatest obstacle is your greatest strength. It took me years to stop fighting this and recognize it as true.

Spiritual Bypassing

People who have been practicing a discipline for a while often assume that the results of practice will carry over into all areas of life. But there is great danger in confusing spiritual attainments with psychological development.

Meditation is not self-help. Buddhism is not self-help. Yoga is definitely not self-help. Though the paths of yoga and meditation can help you see more clearly where you need help in dealing with your issues, they are not a substitute for therapy. The practices help you to see how you get in your own way and cause your own suffering. How to work with these issues is a completely separate approach. From a Buddhist perspective, there is nothing to change. From your spouse's, there might be a different story.

Let's be clear about one crucial point: practice is not the same as doing your psychological work. Practice is training the mind to be present and awake. But it's entirely possible to be a present and awake asshole, if that's how you show up. Practice is about developing awareness, not about resolving your childhood issues.

My former professor, psychotherapist Bruce Tift, describes this dichotomy brilliantly in his book *Already Free*. He identifies two approaches to working with our state of mind: developmental and fruitional. Developmental work is about maturing and learning adult behaviors. Fruitional work is about recognizing open awareness and tolerating it.

The more mature you are, the more openness you can tolerate on both a psychological and a meditative level. Maturity is essentially the ability to tolerate not getting what you want. As an adult you have the capacity to recognize that feelings are not necessarily connected to behavior. You can feel things without acting on them; whereas a child might not yet understand this. If you are not fully matured from a developmental point of view, you might try to control behavior by disconnecting from your feelings. This can have unpleasant side effects on your relationships.

If awareness practices are not helping you to take a look at your habitual patterns, then you are missing out on a big piece of the puzzle.

The hope is that once you become aware that you are an arrogant jerk or a passive aggressive manipulator, you'll take some steps to alter your ways. You might seek therapy to learn how to listen rather than hold court. Or you might need to learn how to speak up for yourself instead of cowering in the face of confrontation. That kind of work is done in a therapeutic setting, not on the meditation cushion.

There is so much marketing out there these days spreading the lie that yoga and meditation will make you a better person. These practices will possibly make you more aware, but it's up to you to choose how—and whether—to act on this awareness.

Spiritual Materialism

A problem with many modern-day approaches to yoga is that, superficially, they promise worldly prizes and easy enlightenment in exchange for learning to become limber through daily physical exercise. When you discover the truth, you may want your money back.

Chögyam Trungpa identified this phenomenon in his book *Cutting through Spiritual Materialism*:

"The problem is that ego can convert anything to its own use, even spirituality. Ego is constantly attempting to acquire and apply the teachings of spirituality for its own benefit."

Walking a spiritual path with a consumer mind-set is like collecting rocks on a backpacking trip. Eventually you're going to have to let them go, or you'll be overburdened and unable to reach your destination. And what the heck are you going to do with all those rocks anyway?

The spiritual path is putting down the rocks of ego so you can carry on lightly, without the weight of baggage, and enjoy the views. Ego in this sense is anything that solidifies your self-image into a fixed identity. You may consider yourself healthy, fit, learned, spiritual, compassionate, or wise, and every one of those characteristics, while noble and potentially beneficial, are ego traps. Because none of it is coming with you in the end, and if you get stuck thinking of yourself as being a certain way, you'll miss out on opportunities for growth.

Marketing encourages all sorts of misconceptions about spiritual practice. We are constantly encouraged to wonder: What Do I Want? The subtext is: And how can this spiritual practice help me get it?

An authentic path to enlightenment does not follow a set of rules or regulations, does not promise instant results, and will be different for each person. You can't buy or bargain your way to happiness through practice.

The point is that an authentic spiritual path is not about creating a version of reality that you can live with. It's about living with the version of reality that you have created—learning to want what you have. This is a tricky one—especially for Americans who have heard from birth that you can have it your way, with a side of fries. Sometimes going deep into practice means not having it your way.

Of course humans in other cultures have their own issues. Each culture creates its own unique set of habitual patterns to work with. I've heard many of my friends from South Asia say that obligation to family leaves no freedom for personal choice. You might say that the American habit is confusing freedom of choice with freedom, plain and simple.

Freedom is earned by slaying demons, not by running away from them or buying them new outfits.

Writing Practice: What Belief Holds You Hostage?

Think about what holds you back or gets in your way. This is your chance to let out all your frustrations. Identify any limiting beliefs or leftover baggage that hold you hostage and free write about it for twenty minutes without stopping.

Use this prompt if you like:

   ✎ What I wish I could change . . .

Now go back through what you just wrote and highlight what you can change. Then brainstorm different ways you could creatively recycle that residue. Be wild, be unreasonable, be helpful. Let your imagination have free rein to come up with illogical connections. How can your trash become beautiful and helpful?

If necessary, repeat.

(Keep this writing exercise as we'll come back to it in the next chapter.)

9

Hopelessness

Disappointment

It's tempting to think that the spiritual path is a linear journey. What a surprise when you see your old neurotic patterns resurfacing again, just like an old dysfunctional relationship you thought you had outgrown. Sometimes it can be painful to look in the mirror and not see growth.

Chögyam Trungpa Rinpoche put this nicely:

> There is a problem in thinking that you are supposed to be advancing in your practice all the time. You don't have to constantly be on the road. If you have a flat tire, that is also part of the journey. Ambition makes you feel that you are not doing anything. There seems to be a hypnotic quality to ambition and speed, so that you feel that you are standing still just because you want to go so fast. You might actually be getting close to your goal.

Often what looks like a disaster or setback is just energy freeing itself up to be available. Haven't you ever had the experience of being devastated by a breakup, only to be grateful, years later, that you moved on?

One of the turning points on my own journey occurred at a lunch in Sarnath—where the Buddha gave his first teaching—with my Swedish–American friend Tara. Strong, poised, and serene, with an ironic smile never far from her lips, Tara was getting ready to be ordained as a nun. We met up one day after the morning teachings we were attending with Thrangu Rinpoche.

I was feeling like a failure because I had not married or settled into a long-term relationship. I kept stubbornly trying to make it work with a man who was wildly unsuitable, because I felt like I needed to have a man in my life. After an animated discussion, I sat glumly playing with my chappati.

She said, "For us independent women on a spiritual path, it often feels like in order to be in relationship with a man, it means giving up the path, or at least toning it down. Most men want a woman at home in the kitchen, or the bedroom, rather than on a prostration board in North India [we had met in Bodhgaya under the bodhi tree when she came to use the prostration board next to mine]. Especially if you have kids, it seems like we have to choose between dedication to family or devotion to a spiritual path. Sure, you can do both, but not with equal intensity. Someone will have to give, and it's not going to be him. If you are devoted to the path, you are going to have to do the giving up."

I felt frustrated and constantly thwarted, like I had a shadow over my head—like a bad luck curse. Yet I had the freedom to devote my time to practice and study. I was in Sarnath studying with realized masters. I could never have done this if I had a husband. And yet I was still complaining.

"I get it," she said. "Why do you think I am taking vows? I told myself that if I had not met my man by age forty that I would start wearing robes. I turn forty this year."

"But the Dalai Lama always says, 'never give up.' Isn't that giving up?" I asked.

"It is giving up on samsara. It's not giving up on life," she said.

I considered this. I didn't want to take vows. I didn't want to shave my head. And I didn't want to wear red robes. Not an option. Good for her, but not for me. This was clear.

But what about acting like it? What about taking that vow internally, to totally dedicate my life to the spiritual path, to waking up? That made sense.

I had found happiness in a life dedicated to spiritual practice, but I still kept looking for a relationship to make me happy. I keep striving for something that had not proven to make me happy, when I had already found something that did. It didn't make sense.

A good gauge of spiritual health is to write down
The three things you most want.
If they in any way differ,
You are in trouble.

—Rumi

I had two longings that were apparently at odds with each other. On the one hand I wanted samsara to go well, I wanted a partner, a comfortable relationship and home. On the other hand, I wanted enlightenment, the total dissolving of ego. There seemed to be a little problem. That problem was this: I wanted.

I think that's the secret. If we want enlightenment we have to give up our most prized hope. Because isn't enlightenment letting go of everything? A death before you die?

Disappointment is a refusal to be with or participate in your life exactly as it is. You create a story that something is missing: you didn't get what you wanted, or you got what you didn't want. Or you had it all, but then it got taken away. Then you interpret this as a lack in your life.

But the "missing element" never existed anywhere but your mind, so is it really missing? Your circumstances are just as they are. Anything that seems missing is simply your interpretation, based on an idea you've come up with.

"Disappointment is the best chariot to use on the path of the dharma," according to Chögyam Trungpa Rinpoche. Disappointment is a necessary stage of the journey. Evolution is not linear. It's more often one step forward, ten steps back. There is no solution to the disappointments you will face in life, except this: your ability to stay with the situation and grow from it. There is no fixing samsara.

Disillusionment

If disappointment is a necessary stage of the path, then disillusionment is really good news. Let me explain.

You have to wear down the mechanism of ego in order for something deeper to arise. It's like you have to get to the end of your rope before you finally leave that bad relationship or job and stop hoping things will change. When you suddenly see the futility of sticking around to work with the situation, you are ready to fly.

Illusion is not reliable. Disillusionment is when you understand this.

Before you can open your mind to new possibilities, you have to be willing to let go of preconceived ideas and history. After all, isn't it illusion that creates confusion? When you hold on to a wishful version of reality that is not corroborated by experience, you perpetuate a false understanding of your world. That's when suffering sets in: your expectations don't align with what's true. Disillusionment gives you the kick in the pants to do something different.

As I write this, the head of the Shambhala lineage—Chögyam Trungpa Rinpoche's son and heir—is being accused of sexual misconduct and has stepped down. The community is in chaos and at least two prominent members committed violent suicide days after the announcement. Many lives were devastated by Sakyong Mipham Rinpoche's actions.

I have nothing personal against the Sakyong—he was always very kind to me. I know he inherited a fantastically difficult situation and he served an important role on my own path. But I want to point out how this whole system of planting a sparkly exotic Eastern religion in the West in the twenty-first century can run amok.

Anytime you systematize something, you take away its life force. It loses its freshness and humanity.

How many times have we heard variations of this story in the past few years?

There seems to be a message here. The paradigm of hierarchical systems ruled by men can be traced back to the crusaders, who outlawed and abolished anything that threatened the authority of the church. Women suspected of secretly accessing spiritual power were burned at the stake. The #metoo movement highlights that things feel out of balance and that society is ready for a change. My sense is that we need to evolve and adapt to the times. Patriarchy might have outlived its days of glory.

In one sense I understand being disillusioned by the disintegration of a community that you call home. It's like losing your family—and I experienced this in the Ashtanga community. I also experienced it early on in Chögyam Trungpa Rinpoche's sangha when the Sakyong created guidelines for his students to follow. It left me very clear: that he was not my teacher, and I moved on to find other teachers to study with. It was heartbreaking to leave my community.

But then I woke up one day and realized that I had to take responsibility for myself and choose my next steps. It's a part of growing and accepting the realities of the world.

I asked Thrangu Rinpoche once what to do since I had connections with two different teachers on each side of a lineage split. I loved his response: just do your practice.

For me this is the main point. I have received teachings and learned practices that I can do for the rest of my life. If the person who taught me does something I question, I still have access to the teaching. I can choose not to learn with that teacher anymore. But if I get caught in a drama as a result of their misconduct, then I am not putting their teachings into practice.

Let me be clear: I have been victim to abuses of power, and I definitely got caught up in the drama! I don't mean to point fingers at those who choose to speak up and incite change. But a useful question might be: How can you learn, let go, and grow from the experience? How can your actions serve to alert, inform, and protect others? What will you become as a result?

Disillusionment is a wake-up call to bring everything back to your practice, back to the path. Onward.

> *Hopelessness is egolessness.*
> —Chögyam Trungpa Rinpoche

Mess

> *As a wind in the mountains*
> *assaults an oak,*
> *Love shook my breast.*
> —Sappho

In order to reorder around a new theme or organizing principle, you have to completely disintegrate. So, at times, your pilgrimage might look and feel like a complete mess. And there is the tiny detail that there is nowhere to get to. No end goal. What, then, is the point?

The point is that when you finally see this, you can stop living life on a roller coaster, getting so excited when things are going well, and then dropping into depression when they stop going well. You start to experience a sense of equilibrium.

You may imagine this would feel like a letdown. Equilibrium sounds flat.

"What's wrong with getting excited when things go well?" you may ask.

There's nothing wrong with being happy—but if you are dependent on external sources for your happiness, then you are going to be in for a wild ride. That ride gets exhausting.

When you are emptied out of all the striving and struggling, you have room to grow. You can start to live in the flow, allowing the rise and fall, the calm and the chaos to come and go without fixating on any of it.

Disintegrating allows for reintegrating in a whole new way.

Why Bother?

Why should you start a yoga and meditation practice? I mean really, why bother? You'll probably alienate your loved ones, invite all the difficult emotions you've spent your life trying to avoid, add one more thing to your already hectic daily to-do list, and probably start analyzing the hell out of everything in your life to see if it aligns with your dharmic path. It's totally inconvenient.

So what is the point?

It's this: When you are able to be aware of and tolerate whatever is going on in the present, you delete an entire layer of suffering in your already stacked layer cake of life. Let's face it: life is hard sometimes.

It's hard enough to handle our own dramas, and now with the Internet we have access to everyone else's as well. It is beyond overwhelming. It's easier to go out and laugh with friends, have a few drinks, smoke, watch a funny movie. Go shopping. Find a new lover.

But what if, instead, you were to take your emotional drama to the yoga mat or the meditation cushion and watch the whole show, start to finish. Sit there in the audience of your own mind. Without popcorn. It doesn't sound so fun, does it? But it is so much better than fun. It is the key to releasing attachment to your storyline—the one that causes you to relive your harrowing drama over and over again.

By sitting still and observing the flow of that story—seeing how it develops according to your expectations, whether you want it to or not—allows you to see your part in the drama. It lets you see how you take part in your own downfall, so you can take responsibility for your character's actions. Then perhaps next time, you can avert the crisis and direct a more peaceful ending to the scene. Eventually, with practice, your perspective shifts to include a wider range of possible outcomes.

A pilgrimage is a self-secret affair. You can't convey that experience fully to another person, even if that person is with you, because it is your experience. The more you talk about your experience, the more you dissipate the energy of it. So there is the wisdom of not talking about it, but there is also the complete inability to share it with another being. Any experience, but especially practice experiences, will always remain your secret. You can share the facts and the feelings, but the whole experience is yours and can never be conveyed in exactly the same way that YOU experienced it.

Depending on how you hold this secret, it either becomes poison or fuel for the path.

No Goal

On one level, this thing we call the spiritual path is simply a structure we give ourselves to stay out of trouble. As in: we're here on the planet and have to do something with ourselves, so it's better to do something helpful rather than harmful. Inevitably, harmful actions will cause suffering. So we train ourselves to be kind.

This then becomes a significant stage of the journey. We get some benefit from our kindness and start to see the workings of cause and effect. The discipline becomes a sort of mirror so that we can witness our development. The danger at this stage is that we start to see some results for our practice, so we start to expect more of the same.

But then somewhere along the way we start to realize that there is no path. *Spiritual path* is just a name for something we see after the fact. It's just your life, moment by moment, lived with integrity. Take the spiritual thinking out of it. No nonsense: nuts and bolts.

The key is to let go of outcomes.

The Heart Sutra (the essence of Buddha's teachings of the second turning, or Mahayana path) reminds us that there is "no eye, no ear, no nose, no body, no mind," and also "no ignorance, no end of ignorance, no end of old age and death, no suffering, no origin of suffering, no cessation of suffering, no path, no wisdom, no attainment and no nonattainment ..."

So what's left?

Anything you can think of is a product of your conceptual mind. And conceptual mind is not the same as wisdom. When you sit down to meditate, you invite wisdom. But in order to do that, you have to give up the idea that there is a goal to attain.

There is no goal. The instruction is this: when you sit down to meditate, invite wisdom and practice dwelling in that wisdom.

In this light, the great Buddhist saint Tilopa left us this provocative reminder:

One should resist, or let go of the temptation, which at some point always arises in the experience of beginning meditators, to improve or make better one's meditation by meditating on tranquility, or on the experience of emptiness, or on clarity, or on bliss, or by fabricating or contriving any other strategy to improve one's meditation. All such attempts to improve one's meditation by "meditating" are obstacles to meditation.

But this may not help ease your mind when you are feeling lost, alone, and discouraged.

I just want to reassure you that hopelessness, disappointment, and disillusionment are part of the path. Just because you feel hopeless does not mean you are doing anything wrong. It might mean you are doing something right, finally.

But it can be a tricky and demoralizing phase of the journey. Read on for an emergency guide on those occasions when you are feeling particularly lacking in motivation.

Three Steps to Get from Stuck to Unstuck

Hopelessness, disappointment, disillusionment, and disintegration are part of the path. When your motivation wanes, you get stuck at the halfway point, or when you lose your way, let this be your guide:

1. **Commit or Recommit to Meditation Practice**
   When you practice training the mind to be present, you learn to focus on what matters to you. This can be taken in an absolute or a relative sense. Could we say the ultimate purpose of life is to be present, relaxed, and happy? Training your mind through meditation can help you to do that. But if you forget your intention, it's easy

to get distracted by the onslaught of thought that often terrorizes the mind and catapults us into fear.

These days, with so much information coming at us nonstop every day, it can be overwhelming to remember our intention. Take time every day—even five minutes—to reconnect with the storehouse of wisdom accessible through silent meditation. The answer is inside of you—not out there in some imagined future. Reestablishing a strong daily practice—through perseverance—reminds you of this.

Practice
Learn a simple meditation technique, set a schedule you can maintain, and stick to it. See the Resources section for an introduction to meditation and tips on how to maintain a regular meditation practice.

2. **Set an Intention**
Developing a mindfulness practice also helps you recognize what your worldly goals are—it allows you to check in with the body and mind to identify where you are in or out of alignment with what you know to be true. It allows you to recognize the path your life wants to take. The practice here is to identify what will make your heart truly happy, so learn to identify that feeling.

Get clear on what you want, even if you have no idea how you are going to get there. Reevaluate influences that may constrict your ability to thrive and consider alternatives. Persevering in practice helps you focus your energy to realize your goals once this

secondary intention is identified. You start to see what
(and who) is not supporting you, so you can let go of
what is holding you back. Practice also has the benefit
of refining your focus so you can stay on task as each
step toward your goals is realized.

Practice
Set a new affirmation for yourself for one week, even
a small one such as, "I'm content in this moment with
whatever is going on" or an intention like, "I will practice
being mindful and present throughout the day." When
you wake up in the morning, first thing, call to mind
your intention or affirmation. Just before you go to bed
each evening, reflect on your progress and feel good
about that. If you lapsed in your efforts, forgive yourself
and set the intention again for the following day. Repeat
every day for one week. Simple tool, powerful results.

3. **Show Up**
Ninety-nine percent of success is simply showing up.
When I first started practicing yoga and confronted
difficult asanas, some days I had no idea where I was
headed. I didn't know how to start approaching it, what
it should feel like. But I persevered, stayed open to the
process and was willing to try new things. Eventually I
would get a clue: a bodily sensation that told me I was
on to something, or suddenly I would be able to move
more deeply into a posture. Things would suddenly
shift in a dramatic way.

Many days it felt like nothing was happening, like
there was no progress at all. Through perseverance, one

day, it happened, like the first day I was able to jump back (a challenging movement in the Ashtanga Yoga sequence). Those weeks, months, and sometimes years of prep time were necessary, even though they often felt frustratingly devoid of any signs of progress.

Commitment is key.

Chögyam Trungpa Rinpoche talks about the gradual path to sudden enlightenment. The art of perseverance has to do with commitment. When you are committed to something or someone, it is like a laser that cuts through all the garbage. You pay less attention to the distractions that threaten to sway you off course (distractions like thoughts and judgments about the situation). You become more focused on the journey. It's not a chore, but a choice. You can turn down the volume on the background noise and instead focus your attention upon whatever it is you choose.

Life is never a linear progression. It's more like two steps forward, three steps back; one step forward eight steps back; twelve steps forward. And then you get a flat tire. We progress in increments, often far too slow for our lumbering or hyperactive mind to recognize as anything remotely satisfying.

Practice

Identify one concrete step forward to take you to the next stage of development, one step at a time toward your goal. Then commit!

When you get thrown to the ground, perseverance is developing the muscle to stand back up again. This not only builds strength and character but also trains you to remain humble. You develop that strength by repeatedly pushing yourself up off the floor.

The situations of fear that exist in our lives provide us with stepping stones to step over our fear. On the other side of cowardice is bravery. If we step over properly, we can cross the boundary from being cowardly to being brave.

—Chögyam Trungpa, *Shambhala:*
The Sacred Path of the Warrior

When you confront fear head-on through remaining present with it, you invite light to shine through. Perseverance enables you to share your gifts with the world, in the form of love. Your love is your gift.

Writing Practice: Dealing with Disappointment

- ✎ What is your biggest regret or disappointment?
- ✎ What ineffective or harmful strategies have you developed to cope with that disappointment?
- ✎ What is the hidden benefit of your participation in that disappointment?

Go back to your previous writing from chapter 8, "What I wish I could change." With a different color, highlight what you can't change.

Write (speaking to things that you can't change): *What I need to accept is...*

10
Letting Go

The Pathless Path

Pilgrimage is like a spiritual path without a map. It's not just following a spiritual tradition—there is a sense of striking out on your own and not knowing what to expect, like the Buddha leaving the comfort of his palace.

Losing reference points can cause panic. Ego has huge resistance to this.

Here's the tricky part: as soon as you decide to quit ego's game of striving for success, and aim toward spiritual pursuits, the ego immediately gets on board. Ego is like a high-tech spy, and knows everything about you even before you do. And if you try to go behind its back, it rises for revenge. It does not like to be left out of the loop.

So as soon as you see through samsara's game and yearn for a closer connection—to the Divine, or God, or Enlightenment—ego will start appropriating the new values. So ego will strive to be more humble and compassionate and holy. I'm sure you've seen this. You can feel when someone is genuinely humble and kind. Conversely you can feel when someone is pretending humility or being kind because they want you to see them as a pious person. It's sticky, like getting honey on your fingers. Truth is not sticky.

My point is that it's really hard to find your own Truth if you are too concerned about following someone else's rules—how to behave, who to revere, what to believe, etc.

I saw this so often in both the yoga and Buddhist communities. Who has the most beautiful yoga asana practice or knows the rituals most precisely? Who is closest to the teacher and sees them socially? Who has the most stylish yoga pants, or—here's a good one—the best ass? Who has done the most advanced practice, or spent the most time in solitary retreat? Or who has the greatest teacher? It's so easy to confuse worldly signs of success with spiritual attainment. We all fall for it.

It's ridiculous. These external references have nothing to do with the quality of a person's practice. Only that person knows, (and perhaps her teacher) and it has nothing to do with how big her Instagram following is or how often she's been featured on the cover of *Yoga Journal*.

A New Story

Being a pilgrim is about releasing your old story and writing a new one. Or rather, a new story writes itself. Your life gets a revision. Sometimes it happens gradually, sometimes you get the direct download.

My so-called boyfriend had stood me up—again—in Bodhgaya. I was there waiting for a new work visa and my return flight to Bhutan to carry on with another season of teaching. I went to sit under the Bodhi Tree to watch my mind and tend to my heart.

Why do I hold on to nonrelationships, I wondered? It was a familiar story, being left hanging by a man I loved. I was at the end of my rope. Enough was enough.

The Hinayana Buddhist teachings say don't get drawn into anger. Anger = Bad. Forgiveness and Kindness = Good. But the situation demanded something stronger. I'd practiced so much forgiveness and patience and kindness that I was starting to feel like a schmuck. And I was TIRED of it. What about kindness and forgiveness toward myself?

So much for peacefulness under the Bodhi Tree. I was agitated, hopeless, and exhausted. Was this whole journey just a waste of time? I didn't feel any wiser or compassionater [sic] than when I started out on this path decades ago. I was irritable and depressed. So tired of heartbreak. And all the pilgrims. We were all doing our little thingy—our prayers and rituals and yogas and mudras and still acting out our neurotic tendencies, and for what? I felt intolerant. Tired of everybody's trip. Their story. My story. Their endless questions:

"Where are you from?"

"Where are you going?"

"Where is your husband?"

Good questions: no fucking clue!

I'd spent so much time confused about what to do. I felt a passion to help all beings stop suffering, but I couldn't seem to get beyond my own. I didn't know how to put the teachings into practice. I had taken the bodhisattva vow to help alleviate suffering in the world. How could I help all sentient beings stop suffering when I was such a goddamn mess?

Sitting with my mental chaos, I surveyed the monks, wondering if they stewed in messy emotions. Why are emotions so inconvenient, so taboo? What is so embarrassing about our inner lives? I prayed for relief from stinking thinking. I whined in my journal and watched the pilgrims.

Such fanfare we create around the search for peace and happiness. The variety of rituals astounded me. Everyone had a thingy: music, flashing lights, candles, paper lanterns, flags, water bowls, bunches of bananas, clumps of onions, fragrant flowers, sprits of perfume, pure white clothing, all red clothing, long unruly dreadlocks, neatly shaved scalps, reverent glances.

Some think all this fanfare will bring us closer to the divine and we tend to imbue it all with such seriousness. Or we go the other route and have partners, children, houses, and jobs; buy appliances and go camping on the weekend. All the roles we play to deny temporarily or forever that this thing we look frantically for out there is not out there at all. It is nowhere else but where we are, right here at any given moment quietly waiting to be uncovered by the fanfare with which we cover it.

I wanted to shout to all the pilgrims that the truth lies behind all of these things. "PEOPLE! We are all dying, don't you get it? Let's just be kind to each other until that day comes."

The Thai monks had taken over the chanting. It always sounded to me like Aaron Neville and his Down on the Bayou style.

> Waah waaaaa wuh waaaahaaaa whaaaaaaaa
> Yellow moon, yellow moon,
> why you keep peeping in my window?
> Do you know something I don't know?

I had this erroneous idea that the spiritual path was all about love and light and peace and calm and radical acceptance. Sure. The END of the path. Once we've gone through all the crap. I kept wondering about K. Pattabhi Jois's promise:

"Do your practice and all is coming."

Heartbreak was coming. Insecurity and fear: coming.

Happiness? Not coming.

"Where is my happiness?" I demanded, unhappily.

Couldn't I walk the path to enlightenment AND have a partner? Must I bow down to a man for both?

In *The Torch of Certainty*, Jamgon Kongtrul wrote:

> "There is no harm in being driven by self-disgust. Meditate unhappily."

No problemo.

I could manage that. And I did.

Incessant mosquitoes, flies, and gnats buzzed in a black cloud around me, making me feel like Pigpen. I was swimming in nihilistic tendencies. How many of us would ever have a glimpse of realization? Even those of us who tried diligently, how much did this help? It felt totally hopeless.

I sat under the bodhi tree all afternoon. Not out of devotion, but because I couldn't fathom anything else to do. Nothing inspired me to get up. I sat all evening, heavy-hearted and beyond despair. Absolute Couldn't Care Less.

That night, hours and hours later, still sitting under the Bodhi Tree with a tear-stained face, flocks of green parakeets chirping in the trees and a faint wet smoke hanging in the darkening air, I let go. It just happened. Abandon any hope of fruition, the slogan goes.

Okay, I said. *I give up.*

I sat as my whole being shook, and prepared to accept what I did not want. Because I finally realized there was no other choice.

I surrendered.

I shuddered in a wet puddle of tears late into the night, hungry and cold, alone in a strange land, grateful to the darkness for hiding my shame.

Not What You Think

When you finally have an insight that changes your world, it's not remotely what you thought it would be. We might expect a spiritual insight as a ray of light from the heavens, or like cupid's playful arrows. In fact, it's more like being cupid's target—you think it's going to be so cute and fun!—and then realize those fuckers are real and you're bleeding profusely.

For the ego, it's not a pretty picture. For the mind, however, it is like realizing the prison gates are open. You suddenly realize you can walk right through them. Because it is all an illusion, a big gigantic dream. Empty of anything permanent and lasting. Like a moon on water or a rainbow or a plate of chocolate chip cookies left out on the counter. Gone when you look again.

Truth is not found by being good or obedient or chaste, by making offerings or chanting prayers. There is no formula for waking up.

When you finally realize there is nothing to lose, because you are going to lose everything in the end or that you have already lost it, then something else arises. Something lighter. Life is but a dream: merrily merrily. Or not.

I realized that evening under The Tree that if I continued to maintain the whiny grasping mentality I would be miserable forever. I thought to myself, *Okay. I know this one already. Let's try something new.*

The Good News

The good news is that, after getting annihilated, you realize you can handle anything because in fact, "you" and "anything" are essentially the same.

I flew to Bangkok—where I would catch my flight to Paro—and splurged for a suite so I could enjoy my last bubble bath for another three months. Afterward, I sat at a sushi bar and ate salmon rolls (purring slightly), then walked to the market for some fruit. There are so many different varieties of luscious fruit in Thailand; it's like Candyland. I was sipping fresh passionfruit juice from a straw as I made my way out of the crowded market. I put my shopping bag down for a moment to adjust my straw. I picked up my bag again, glanced up as I took a step forward and almost ran smack into a man. I stopped cold with a jolt.

I knew this man. He had just stood me up in Bodhgaya.

My heart raced. I dropped my bag. My mind whirled and went blank as blood rushed to my face. I wondered if I was dreaming. We stared. I considered poking him to see if he was real. He had a strange golden hue about him. A good minute passed. We stared some more, mouths open. He laughed. I smiled and shook my head. We had not seen or spoken to each other in over a month. I thought he was still in India.

"I would give you a hug but I am contagious," he said. "I had to go to the emergency room. I got hepatitis."

It was true. He was yellow.

It was the proverbial carrot—dangling in my face. But I didn't want the carrot anymore. I was finished with carrots. Finished with vegetables, finished eating, for that matter. Fasting. And so I didn't know how to relate to this man who seemed to pop up in my life over and over and pull me into a hot little Latin dance and then leave again. My head was spinning from India, my heart was numb from disuse or abuse—not sure which; in any case from not being used properly. I was ready to go back to Bhutan to my peaceful solitary hermit's life.

But you have to keep on going. There is no stopping the treadmill. It's either keep moving or get your pant leg stuck in the teeth.

He took me to his favorite restaurant near the river. He wanted to visit me in Bhutan. Neither of us could afford to pay the daily visa fee (mine was included in my employment contract), and I didn't have the connections to get him in without a visa. I didn't have a home anywhere, and neither did he.

There was nothing to do but let go.

Accepting Aloneness

Somewhere along the way, pilgrimage introduces you to your aloneness. We come here alone, we will leave alone. Since the bulk of modern culture proposes everything under the sun to deny this basic fact of existence, continuing to practice is an act of defiance.

Alone = All One. We are allone. At times this can be hard to bear. But my experience is that the voice of inner wisdom gets louder when we can tolerate our aloneness.

Society has dictated certain goals for you, as if your life was laid out before you were even born: find a partner, make babies, find a way to support yourself in a consumer culture and be happy ever after. When these goals elude you, or when you choose not to embrace them, the fundamental truth of aloneness can feel like a curse—like being banished to the forest with an "A" embroidered on your sweater.

At a certain point, I finally saw the depth of my confusion. I had to admit that I had no discriminating awareness when it came to relationships. I wanted so badly to be loved, that I ignored whatever didn't support that scenario. I could not see the truth. I failed to see my own participation in the dynamics because I was so intent on getting what I wanted. I wanted someone to prove to me that I was worthy of love. Because I did not love myself.

I learned that I had to extend love and respect, compassion and forgiveness to myself before I could receive it from anyone else. I had so often denied myself this self-respect. I vowed to make that part of my practice.

Your greatest obstacle is your greatest gift. My singleness turned out to be the biggest boon, allowing me the freedom to pursue my spiritual path and a vocation that I was passionate about. But I had so much fear of being judged for what I perceived as a lack that I couldn't recognize my obstacle as a gift. My shame clouded my light.

Power Places

Pilgrimage is about a journey. For most of us, that journey takes place on Earth. Nature is our witness and place plays a key role. Power places can help accelerate your growth.

There are many ways land can be imbued with power. Crestone, Colorado, is said to be a power place, both because of its native American history as sacred ground, but also because of the geology and energetic "ley lines" that apparently converge here. In India, Bodhgaya—especially the area around the bodhi tree where the Buddha attained enlightenment—and Deer Park, where the Buddha gave his first teaching, are power places. Tibetan lore acknowledges the presence of hidden lands—*beyul*—that are "places where physical and spiritual worlds overlap and Tantric practice effectiveness increases with multiple perception dimensions."[10]

Power places are like holes in the enveloping fabric of material existence. The veil feels thinner, like the unseen world is just a bit closer. You sense that there is something happening "behind the scenes" and would not be surprised to see the unexpected. They open up a space in which you can connect with spirit guides and with the source of sacred wisdom.

Because power places attract and hold energy there is also the possibility to dissolve obstacles more quickly, thus speeding up the process of karma. Everything—including obstacles—is heightened.

One of the most mysterious power places is the tiny Himalayan Kingdom of Bhutan. A land fiercely loyal to its traditions and closed to the outside world until 1974, the national religion is Vajrayana Buddhism. So there is a certain magic to life in Bhutan.

My friends managed a luxury resort in Paro, the second-largest town. When they invited me to come teach for three months, I dropped everything.

Life in Bhutan is incredibly slow. People move in rhythms redolent of historic agrarian cultures. With a population of six hundred thousand, yaks were more common than humans. I often walked around expecting to see Frodo or a donsy of gnomes. The most striking feature of Bhutan is an indescribable richness in the atmosphere, an energetic field much like the negative ions you experience before a thunderstorm, only different. It's like you feel something in the air, but you don't know what it is. It's like you notice there is something in the air that you can't explain.

One day I walked past the hotel's conference room, serious chairs surrounding an important table, and I had a moment of insight. The scene contrasted so starkly to the surrounding rice fields, filled with extended family and neighbors, all camped out in the paddies, harvesting the family wealth with medieval tools. Next to this, business deals and big finance felt so extraneous, so totally irrelevant as a sustainable way of life.

I once heard it said that if you reduced the dharma teachings into one word, that word would be, "relax." Something about being in Bhutan inspired this relaxation—an awakening and opening, or at least a softening of preconceived ideas. As one hotel guest put it, "This is the kind of place one comes to make major life changes."

That is one of the characteristics of a power place.

This is not to say you can't have powerful experiences in "non-power places." You can. You will have the exact experience you need to propel you along your path, no matter where you are in the world.

While I was in Paro, I finished a set of practices that I had been working on for over a year. I was thrilled to be finished, and a bit relieved. The same day, I received an e-mail that unleashed the most inexplicable and excruciating series of events—to this day it remains one of my hardest trials. My boyfriend—though he had not yet told me—had met his future wife. But when that e-mail came through, I just knew.

Another characteristic of a power place—they speed up your karmic lessons. That's another way of saying the closer you get to realization the bigger the obstacles get. Sometimes that might look like your world is falling apart.

A Map to Reinvent Yourself When Things Fall Apart

1. Take stock and identify support: Let go immediately of what wants to dissolve. The sooner you are able to let go of something weighing you down, the better. Allow space for something new to arrive.

2. Preserve resources: Stop spinning your wheels and reflect on the new landscape. This is when I usually schedule a meditation retreat. Make friends with space and try not to fill it up.

3. Solitude and silence are needed for creation: Notice the visions of your life that arise, whether or not you think they are realistic. What do you really want? Where does your heart tell you to go? Sometimes big breaks can give you permission to do what you've always wanted to do. You can't rush this phase, so let it arrive in its own sweet time.

4. Take one small step in any direction: Just one step, for now. A life-changing journey begins with one small step.

Writing Practice: What Are You Holding On To?

- What is the one thing you think you cannot handle— your worst nightmare that you have been trying to avoid your whole life?
- Do you have a life plan that absolutely must work out?
- Are you afraid of letting go of a cherished dream?
- Can you imagine how your life would look if you suddenly lost everything?

11

Guidance

~~

Finding a Teacher

When the student is ready, the teacher appears. Although you may have to exert a bit of effort to meet halfway.

Since I had relegated Ashtanga to the back burner, I wanted to complete the foundation practices of the Vajrayana. So I needed to find a teacher. I went to Nepal to attend a three-month retreat at a monastery outside of Boudhanath, in Kathmandu.

Did I mention that part of preparing for higher teachings usually involves some sort of test?

The political situation in Nepal, which had been deteriorating for the past two decades due to the Maoists' upsurge, was creating chaos on all fronts. Infrastructure, never one of Nepal's strong points, was falling apart. Load sharing limited our electricity to about eight hours a day—usually in the wee hours—and it was February in the Himalaya. Ice crystals formed inside the windows of my small dark room. I wore all of my clothes: four sweaters, two pairs of socks, hat, and gloves, day and night. There was a severe petrol shortage, which meant we could not fuel the generators at the monastery when the power was out. Bathing in ice water was torture, so I basically stopped doing it. It was too extravagant to use generators for lights or hot water—we needed to ration generator fuel for the kitchen, so we could eat.

When not practicing or listening to teachings, I shivered under the covers with my headlamp, reading the *Uttaratantra Shastra*—the text we were studying. There was talk of sending us home, as we could not get food deliveries. For a few days the borders were closed due to the chaos. All seventy-five of us in the program got sick. It is said that karma ripens more quickly in Jambudvipa—the mythic name for the Indian subcontinent. At least (I hoped) the karma was getting purified. Now if I could just find a guru.

The Great Stupa of Dharmakaya is said to grant wishes to those who ask with faith and devotion. One day, walking around the "wish fulfilling" stupa,[11] wishing for a teacher to guide me, I was shocked awake by a realization. I suddenly realized, as the blood rushed to my head: I already had a teacher. He lived a one-minute walk from where I stood. All at once I understood the significance of power places.

I had totally forgotten that seven years earlier, while I was working on the study abroad program in Kathmandu, I went to see Thrangu Rinpoche one afternoon and asked him to be my teacher. He had smiled brightly, sat up straight, and said, "I accept." And I promptly forgot about it because I became so focused on the Ashtanga yoga practice all those years.

I hurried to finish my circumambulation and went directly to his monastery. I asked one of the monks if I could see Rinpoche. He told me to come back early the next morning.

Making the traditional offerings to Thrangu Rinpoche the next morning, I was welcomed into his private room with his radiant smile. I was stunned at my rapid climb from mental poverty the previous day, to sitting alone with one of the most respected masters of Tibetan Buddhism. It all had the effect of making me feel like I was moving in a dream.

I confessed how much trouble I was having finishing prostrations. Some people finish the whole program in a year or two. It had been ten years since I received the empowerment at the Vajrayana seminary to embark on that path, and I had barely begun. I was already exhausted and physically drained from teaching yoga, much less trying to keep up my own intense Ashtanga practice. I simply had not had enough energy to add another grueling physical practice on top of it.

Thrangu Rinpoche gave me simple advice and suggested I go into retreat. He told me about his new retreat center in Baktapur, just outside of Kathmandu. It cost four dollars a day to stay in a retreat room with private bath, hot water, and three meals a day. So I booked a retreat room for after the Pullahari program, and set a goal to finish ten thousand prostrations. I made a deal with myself: ten days, one thousand prostrations a day; that was my only responsibility. One focus. Just do ten thousand prostrations in ten days. I knew that if I could make this first one happen, then I could schedule ten-day retreats for the rest of the year and finish the practice.

Deepening into Practice

If you stay with the practice and let it affect you, eventually you will be ready to dive deeper. An authentic lineage will offer this possibility. In the zen tradition you would get koans that are increasingly challenging. In Ashtanga, there are some crazy difficult postures that come in the advanced series, but before you can get there, you have to complete the primary and intermediate series. The Tibetan Buddhist path restricts certain teachings to those who have completed the preliminary practices.

The special preliminaries, *ngondro* in Tibetan, are a set of foundational practices that pave the way to more advanced practices on the Vajrayana path. They consist of four different practices done in sequence, and aspiring tantrikas[12] complete one hundred thousand of each.

The first set of one hundred thousand is a physical practice—prostrations—accompanied by a visualization and short mantra. Prostrations are like fast sun salutations—hands up to the forehead, then to the throat, then to the heart, then throw the body down prone on the board, extend the arms completely, count one bead on the mala, then back up. This is how to purify oneself to receive higher teachings. It is utterly exhausting, and though I had a fairly strenuous yoga practice, prostrations felt more like a marathon. I suppose this is the point—to become completely exhausted with conditioned existence.

I completed the bulk of my one hundred thousand prostrations at the Maha Bodhi Temple in Bodhgaya, surrounded by red-robed Tibetans completing their own set for the second or third (or tenth) time. Hundreds of pilgrims on wooden prostration boards—flat rectangles of wood, like simple doors without hardware—crowded the lawn surrounding the temple. The monks devised all sorts of tricks to make the process easier, and I quickly learned from them. We elevated the far end of our boards on bricks to reduce the angle of decline. We stitched together (or purchased from local vendors) layers of fishing net to use as hand pads to reduce friction against the board. We piled thick cotton mats under our knees and chest so the descent was not so brutal. It took me weeks to perfect the technique to minimize pain, but I never eliminated it entirely. I walked with a limp the entire time. I found ways to cope, but I cursed and cried a lot too.

Once prostrations are completed (a moment that marks a celebratory milestone) the practitioner goes on to complete one hundred thousand recitations of the Vajrasattva mantra, then the same number of mandala offerings and guru yoga mantras. There are complicated and precise rituals and liturgy to accompany each of these practices, and the whole ngondro can take years to complete.

You need a teacher to give permission and a formal transmission to begin the practice. There's an exchange that happens between teacher and student—sort of like lighting a candle from someone else's flame. It has to start somewhere; you can't just magically poof your own fire at the beginning. So there is a thread of wisdom that gets passed down from teacher to student. The Sanskrit word *tantra* actually means "strand or thread in a weaving." It's as if the student gets woven into the fabric of the wisdom lineage, and helps to keep it alive.

Chögyam Trungpa Rinpoche had been my original inspiration, but I never met him live and in person. Although I did receive permission to do these practices from his lineage—during a three-month Vajrayana seminary in Colorado—I needed a living teacher to guide me. Devotion is a key element of tantric Buddhism—you can't bypass the guru in Vajrayana.

They call the Vajrayana path the quick path to enlightenment. Because it's the most direct route, it's also the most dangerous. Just like climbing a mountain, you can go slow and steady on a gradual winding path—the Hinayana or Theravada path Buddhism—taking years, or lifetimes, to reach the top. Or you can just hike straight up, bushwacking through bears' dens. If you're fearless and strong and smart, you might make it. Or you might get mauled. But for those of us with a reckless urge to wake up to the truth, there really is no other choice.

Guru or Guide?

There's a big difference between a guide and a guru. A guide can share practices and resources with you but may not have full realization, so he or she cannot take you all way to the full fruition of the spiritual path.

Guru literally means "heavy." It indicates someone who has not only experience of walking the path, but also realization of the nature of mind. He has the gravitas to hold the lineage seat and share the teachings.

You may spend most of your time studying with your guide: your kalayanamitra, or spiritual friend. Gurus are often busy people and you may or may not get to meet with them individually. A guide may have time to sit with you and get to know you personally. But a guru has the insight and experience to fearlessly direct you to your own wisdom.

What happens around an authentic guru is that mind tunes in on a much more subtle level than usual—you start to notice with more precision the subtle signs that come from the phenomenal world.

This process operates on the theory of resonance. Thought waves affect more course waves (of physical matter) and change the mood of the surrounding environment. Anyone who experiences this shift vibration will alter their own vibration to resonate with the more refined waves. This is how a guru can change the mind of a student. And why following a teacher is a requirement for the Vajrayana path. (And also why it's so important to pay attention to who you spend time with.)

There is an atmosphere around an authentic guru that helps show you the illusory nature of the hopes and dreams that make up the mental landscape of your reality. Progressing on the spiritual path is not about getting what you want: the guru is not interested in helping you to fulfill your worldly goals. He will steer you toward the lessons that you need most in order to purify the obscurations that hide the brilliance of mind. Then maybe your worldly goals will be fulfilled, but this is not the main point. This is all really hard to do without an authentic teacher to mirror your experience.

Because the Vajrayana practices are transmitted exclusively from guru to student in an unbroken lineage, it is imperative to have a teacher. But even if your guru shows you the nature of mind, you still have to recognize it yourself. Ultimately you must discover your own source of light.

Learning to Say No

Part of good guidance means learning to say no to situations and people that impede your growth. This is where the Buddhist teachings on compassion can get confusing. Part of compassion is learning healthy boundaries. It means respecting yourself enough to discover what supports your spiritual growth and letting go of what doesn't. This is a big lesson for some of us.

As a woman, I had a tendency to keep giving and forgiving, even when it was no longer appropriate. I would do anything to avoid confrontation. I wanted to be nice—not because I particularly wanted to be nice—but because I couldn't stand being scolded, yelled at, or criticized. I would rather have done anything, even be treated disrespectfully, than initiate a fight.

And I conveniently fit this neurotic behavior into a nice package and called it compassion. I distorted all those Buddhist teachings on kindness so I could smugly justify my inability to speak up. I was a yes girl.

Apparently Warren Buffet once said, "The difference between successful people and really successful people is that really successful people say no to almost everything." This baffled me for a while. Wouldn't saying yes open more doors and allow for more opportunities to arise?

But then this is the problem. Too many choices often lead to indecision or inaction. No clearly defines your territory. No is confidence that you don't need to jump at every new thing. No means: my well-being is a priority.

Have you ever found yourself in one of these situations?

- Saying yes when you really want to say no
- Feeling guilty for saying no
- Keeping silent when someone doesn't treat you well
- Giving too much in an effort to be liked or valued
- Not speaking up when someone does something rude or inappropriate
- Doing something against your will in order to keep the peace
- Assuming that people will know what you are thinking without you having to say what's on your mind.

Why is it so hard for some of us to set boundaries? If you never had boundaries set for you as a child, you might not know how to set them as an adult. Some parents are just not that involved, or they never learned for themselves the value of imposing limits.

If you were punished each time you stood your ground as a child, you might fear rejection if you try to set boundaries. You might equate boundaries with confrontation. You might get the mistaken impression that the way to earn love and respect from others is to be compliant. Saying yes is fine if it's in alignment with your values. But saying Yes because you are too scared to say No doesn't earn anyone's respect, least of all your own.

To learn effective boundaries, you need to recognize what makes you feel good and what makes you feel bad. The only way to identify that is to be in touch with your feelings—which are accessed through the body. If this is not your strong point, fear not. Boundaries are a skill set that can be learned.

The Benefits of Setting Boundaries

The first step in setting boundaries is to identify your needs. If you are a people pleaser and dependent upon public opinion for your self-confidence, even this might be new territory. You might have to give yourself permission to acknowledge your needs and disappoint people. Setting boundaries is about protecting your state of mind from disturbing influences.

1. **Saying No**
   When you are able to say No to people and situations, it shows you can take good care of yourself. Boundaries affirm where you stand in relation to the world. They allow you to filter your experiences—to a certain degree—so that you can avoid unnecessary pain and suffering. Boundaries are like gatekeepers, selecting who and what you want in your inner circle.

2. **Define Your Boundaries**
   Setting boundaries is how we define ourselves. We lay down the foundation of what will be allowed in and what we want to keep out. We allow things into our inner circle that we deem helpful, safe, healthy, or conducive to our growth.

Setting boundaries means saying NO. That means actively choosing and selecting what we say YES to. Healthy boundaries are permeable—not too tight and not too loose. Firm, but adaptable.

How do you define your own boundaries and how do you enforce them? Speak up? Retreat? Take legal action? Ask?

3. **Boundaries Define Relationships**

Boundaries are kind—we show our care by setting boundaries. Meditation practice is important to me, so when I am practicing, I turn my phone off and ask friends not to interrupt me so that I can focus. I care about my health, so I say NO when someone offers me a cigarette. Boundaries allow us to prioritize what we want more of in our lives. It also allows the people in your life to trust you. People like to know where they stand, so communicating boundaries lets them know.

Setting boundaries is sane. It shows that we are sturdy and stable and know how to take care of ourselves. Without boundaries, you just float through life like a leaf blown by the wind. You'll accept anything.

You can practice setting boundaries in small ways. Practice saying No to get used to the feelings it brings up.

4. **Boundaries and Guilt**

If you are afraid to disappoint people, you might feel guilty setting boundaries. If that's a problem for you, you might need to learn to work with your guilt.

Setting boundaries clears space and this can be uncomfortable. Some people get nervous if there is too much space. They want to fill it up with words or activity or people or accomplishments or anything under the sun to avoid confronting space. But space is a great healer. If guilt comes up for you, allow it space.

Recognize that healthy aggression is normal. By listening to it you know when it is appropriate to set a boundary.

5. **Trust Yourself**

Saying No when it is appropriate shows you can take personal responsibility for whatever is happening in the moment. You take care of yourself based on needs and priorities that are current.

Boundaries show self-respect. When boundaries are ignored or denied, we learn that our integrity is not important. This can have profound and devastating effects. Marking the boundaries of your territory allows you to define what comes in and what is not invited into your focus.

Boundaries are important for mental health and learning to take care of yourself. If you are a people pleaser, you can spend your whole life pleasing others at the expense of your own happiness. When you try to make everyone happy, you usually end up making no one happy. So it's to everyone's advantage to practice "effective selfishness."

6. **Be Patient**

Setting boundaries allows the space necessary for transformation to occur. You wouldn't expect a new relationship to thrive without setting aside some quality time. Relationships need nourishing. You need privacy to delve deep into things. This is also true for your practice—you are developing your relationship with your inner wisdom. So forgive relapses and be patient as you learn a new skill.

Checklist

Here's how to set healthy boundaries:

1. Identify your needs.
2. Define your boundaries.
3. Communicate your boundaries.
4. Recognize and allow guilt that may arise.
5. Trust yourself.
6. Be patient.

Boundaries establish your limits. When you shift your awareness from external to internal reference points, you reaffirm the connection with your inner wisdom. This relationship is like any other—it thrives when we make it a priority.

A Note on Technology

Part of setting boundaries these days includes technology usage. This one development is probably the most invasive influence on developing a meditation practice. The challenge is to maintain mindfulness and awareness while being constantly distracted. It's almost impossible to stay focused on the elusive object of meditation when you've got buzzers and beeps and news of the whole world inches from your meditation cushion. So one way to adapt with the times is to consider this as a practice as well.

Discipline yourself to stay away from technology for a certain period of time on a regular basis. It's up to you how you interpret this. It may mean:

- Do not look at anything with a screen before 9:00 a.m.
- Go completely off-grid all day on Sundays.
- Go dark for an entire month.
- Write a list of guidelines for your own use of technology. Just as you might want to limit unhealthy food or other habits in your life, how often, when and where do you want to use your smartphone or computer? What limits do you want to set?

Writing Practice: What Would Your Inner Wisdom Say?

At a certain point, our inner wisdom becomes trustworthy and we have access to the "inner guru." Ironically, this is often when a teacher appears.

Think of a question you want to ask your spiritual guide or teacher. Then write as if you were that teacher giving you advice.

- Write longhand and let out all your confusion, doubts, and questions you'd like to ask about your life and the direction your life is taking.
- Then write for twenty minutes as if you were the wise teacher responding.

Part 3

Coming Home

April 2009
Paro, Bhutan

Sitting on the concrete front step of my small studio, halfway up a mountain, I am watching the sun set over the vast Paro valley below. A wild wind whips downvalley, so I snuggle my monk-red pashmina closer around me, flipping it up over the top of my head against the cold. Far below, the Paro Chhu winds its way slowly south toward India, carrying the freshly melted winter snows to lower altitudes. Across the river basin, the Himalayan foothills guard the higher snow peaks hidden by gentle rolling slopes covered in thick blue pine and cypress. Just down the hill from the old Paro Resort that is our employee housing is Paro Dzong, imposing not only in its sheer mass, but also for its magical architectural beauty. Outlined by the pristine landscape beyond, the high-walled fortress looks like something from a seventeenth-century fairy tale. In fact, according to legend, that's exactly what it is.

My cell phone beeps in my fleece pocket and I check it quickly, hoping it's a message from Fabrice. It's not from him. It's from Isabel, with whom I spent the day at Tiger's Nest cave, Bhutan's national treasure. It was my fifth visit there, and today it was simply the two of us, a nice leisurely Sunday stroll up, a picnic lunch, a good girl talk on the hike down. She wants me to join her for dinner downtown. We returned too late for the staff meal so we have to fend for ourselves.

I text her back: "coming," and take the dirt trail in the fading light through the meadow that separates the staff housing from the hotel where we work. She drives us down the mountain in one of the hotel's SUVs, over the bridge and along the wide river until we reach Paro town as dark settles in.

I always feel like I'm driving on to the movie set of a Wild West shoot-'em-up cowboy film when I enter Paro. It's what you might call a two-horse town. Every building is constructed in the traditional architecture—it's the law—so you could easily be in the seventeenth century. Wooden construction with ornate decorations framing doors and awnings and windows—like old ghost towns of the American West—except that they're painted with bright colored accents and the occasional penis. The phallus is said to ward off evil spirits, so locals depicted them—usually spewing copious quantities of their life-giving nectar—prominently on exterior walls next to the entryway.

The entire town consists of two one-way roads about seven blocks long: Main Street with its storefront mercantiles, wine distributors, textile shops, hardware stores, and a few artisan shops for tourists runs west and up valley. The secondary road parallels it, past the Bank of Bhutan, the stinky fruit shop, a couple of restaurants, and the karaoke bar, heading east and out of town, toward Thimpu. Always a few people mill about, but just a few—that's all there are in Paro. Just a few people. In fact that's all there are in all of Bhutan and if you ask a local the population of Bhutan, that is quite possibly the answer you might get: just a few only, Madam.

This morning on our way to the trailhead twenty minutes up valley, we stopped at the weekly market to see if oranges from Punakha district were in season yet. We made a quick tour through the rows of tarps laid out on the bare ground, piled high with chilies, chanterelle mushrooms, potatoes, bitter gourds, asparagus, ginger, walnuts, eggplants. A few vendors had nice-looking broccoli, my favorite, but I don't have a kitchen so it's useless to me. We found a small crop of oranges for sale, the first of the season, and still quite sour, but we got them anyway for the vitamin C, which is hard to come by here. As we were walking back to the car, parked on Main Street, I heard a man sneeze clear across town, seven blocks away.

"Bless you," I said, to no one in particular.

In search of dinner, we park in front of our usual, Sonam Troephel, the best restaurant in town, or more precisely, the only good one. The young girl at the restaurant recognizes us and points us to our favorite corner table. The other three tables in the restaurant are full. A Bhutanese family of six occupies one—an elderly couple, three young children, and a woman probably in her thirties. They are dressed traditionally: kiras, gorgeous wraparound woven dresses in colorful cotton or silk for the women, ghos like thick beautiful knee-length bathrobes, tied at the waist, for the men. They share a meal of red rice, dahl, ema daatsi, mutton curry, serving each other family style and eating with their hands. At another table sit three loud men, also in ghos, exposing hard muscled brown thighs between the hems of their ghos and their black knee socks, happily polishing off a bottle of Bhutan Highland whiskey, smoking black market cigarettes—selling cigarettes is illegal here. In the far corner, a dignified-looking monk in maroon robes sits speaking English quietly and intently over tea with a Western woman, someone Isabel recognizes from Thimpu. They wave at each other from across the small room.

Isabel is Australian by way of Germany, or perhaps the other way around, and has lived in Paro for three years already. You can count on one hand the number of blonde-haired, blue-eyed residents in Paro, so we have a habit of standing out, and by extension, of making friends easily. People are curious.

"Where are you from?" they want to know. "And where are your husbands?"

I look teasingly at Isabel, "Yeah. Where are our husbands?"

"Good question," she replies, rolling her eyes.

We order vegetarian thukpa—handmade noodle soup—and momos, Tibetan dumplings. While we are waiting, we sip hot ginger lemon honey. Tired from our long hike, we stare out the window in silence. Outside, a young couple in western dress—jeans and fleece—crosses the street, laughing.

"Any news from Caveman?" Isabel asks.

Fabrice has spent several months in retreat in a cave in Nepal. He should be coming out soon. Not exactly a convenient relationship.

"Not a peep. 'It's just like that only,'" I say, mimicking the typical Bhutanese response to an unsatisfactory situation.

"That's what they keep saying."

After dinner we stroll to the general store to buy a few supplies since we only come to town once every week or so—tea, biscuits, cashew nuts, top-up credit for our mobile phones. Isabel lives in the room next door to me. After we return home, we take our evening tea and sit quietly on our front steps until bedtime, listening to the breeze and the local dogs, watching the twinkling lights of Paro town and wondering at the strange fate that brought us both to the land of the thunder dragon. From our perch, we have a view of the entire valley.

This vast valley that brings cold wind holds a secret that I've begun to discern. The spirit of Padmasambhava lives in this valley, and if you listen very carefully he will speak to you. He will guide you to ally with the vastness, the spacious, still and silent background, instead of the unending play of the busy mind. If you give him your mind, he will tame it, gentle it, expand it, hand it back to you bigger than space, calmer than the slow-flowing river, so that you won't even recognize it anymore, won't even recognize yourself.

12

Acceptance

~~~~

Coming Home

What happens after you've gone through the journey and the transformation?

Nothing!

There are no bells and whistles, nothing to show what you've gone through. No trophy (unless you've picked up a statue of Manjushri along your travels.) No awards ceremony, no certificate, no diploma, no Doctorate of Pilgrimage. No high fives.

Nada. Zero. Zilch.

Goose eggs.

You'll have nothing to show for yourself.

Ego hates that.

Your people at home will probably still be living the same old boring lives.

Chances are they will ask you very few questions—if any— about your journey and what you've gone through. They're not that interested.

You might come home and, like Dorothy waking up with a bump on her head, wonder if it was all a dream.

After the ecstasy, the laundry, Jack Kornfield offered.

How do you reinhabit your world with a new perspective?

How do you justify your journey when you've come home empty-handed?

Now comes the real work.

> The everyday practice is simply to develop a complete
> acceptance and openness to all situations and emotions
> and to all people, experiencing everything totally without
> mental reservations and blockages, so that one never
> withdraws or centralizes into oneself.
>
> —Dilgo Khyentse Rinpoche

No Prize

There is no prize at the end of the path (and no end to the path).

Or, you could widen your view to see what the real prize is: an absolutely unshakeable experience of the truth of this life, your life, that whatever comes together will fall apart. That you should never for an instant fall into the laziness of believing that what you have will last, or that what looks like a sure thing will turn out as you expect.

Chögyam Trungpa Rinpoche put this nicely: "The bad news is you're falling through the air, nothing to hang on to, no parachute. The good news is, there's no ground."

Perhaps we have to go through the whole game of pretending there is something to achieve or acquire, a goal to attain. But the life you planned for yourself is probably not the plan life has for you.

A friend told me a story.

"We think that when we enter the path of spiritual discipline, that it's like getting on a lifeboat to row to the other side of the river. We think that enlightenment is on the other side, and all we have to do is get in the boat and row row row to the other side. But what happens is that we manage to find a boat, we get halfway across, and the boat sinks," he said.

"And then what?" I asked, urgently.

"Exactly," he said.

This idea that we call "me" is a farce—and one that we base our entire lives on. But it's what we humans do. We conceptualize self as a solid, separate, permanent entity, when the only constant is the fact that things fall apart.

They say enlightenment is the total annihilation of ego, or rather seeing that it never existed in the first place. From the ego's perspective, it doesn't sound that appealing.

When asked how he stayed so even and content, Krishnamurti put it this way, "I don't mind what happens."

Sometimes I put it like this: "I don't give a fuck."

Twenty-First-Century Woman

The opportunities I've had to travel the world and pursue my spiritual practices were unheard of for women even a couple of decades ago. I'm blessed to have been born in an era that allowed me to follow my bliss.

Yet. There is still a pretty clear demarcation in how traditional teachings are disseminated. Men teach, women learn.

Padmasambhava told his consort Yeshe Tsogyal:

The gross bodies of men and women are equally suited,
But if a woman has strong aspiration, she has higher potential.[13]

Yet all but a handful of the teachers I knew of were male. Why?

All the gurus I'd met said that women and men were equal, that women could attain enlightenment just as easily a man. "Everyone is same," they said. But then why did the nuns have a few hundred more vows to take than the monks? And why did they always have to sit at the back of the room during practice? Why were there so many nunneries without funding in Bhutan? Why were there shrines in some of the Bhutanese gompas (monasteries) where women are not admitted?

The first Vajrayana teacher I ever met all those years ago at my first meditation retreat—Khandro Rinpoche—was a woman. She was one of my first inspirations to begin this path. And I have never met—or even heard of—another female rinpoche since. Where are all the women teachers?

I totally respect Khandro Rinpoche, but it feels like a consolatory concession to the Tibetan tradition that there is one recognized woman tulku. Whenever I bring up this subject in Buddhist circles, people are quick to point out, "There is a woman rinpoche, Khandro Rinpoche."

Yes. But she is the only one!

WHY is there only ONE woman Rinpoche?

How do I fit into this whole scene as a woman? How do I make my way? Who said that men were in charge or that men know more than women? Who decided that men rule the world? I'd like to have a word with them.

The problem is that if I, as a woman, speak up about this imbalance then I'm labeled an angry feminist and my voice is discounted. I won't be taken seriously. Because that angry activism doesn't work—no one wants to hear it. There has to be dialogue—or better, action—that both sides can hear—the dissenters need to be able to at least hear your side before you can even hope for a dialogue. Who wants to listen to someone shouting insults in your face to get your attention?

Ultimately it's not just females we need to bring into equality as much as it is feminine wisdom, which men and women both share. The Western world as we know it in the twenty-first century is dominated by the masculine—a paradigm that relies on structure, aggression, conquest, and intimidation. Traditional societies align more with feminine approach, harnessing power through communication, understanding, yielding, and collaboration.

So the implementation of legislation won't help a damn thing in disrupting the patriarchy. Because legislation is a masculine approach to change. Change has to start—as UNESCO's mission statement identifies—in the minds of men, or at least the patriarchal way of thinking. That change happens through listening.

> When a problem is rooted in society's habitual outlook and habitual thinking, then legislating change will have limited effect. After all, you cannot legislate a change in thinking.
> —His Holiness the 17th Karmapa, Ogyen Trinley Dorje

Acceptance versus Improvement

How do you practice acceptance without falling into laziness? Shouldn't we try to improve things when possible?

It's important to distinguish between state of mind and developmental stage. State of mind is what you work with in meditation practice—it is the quality of your awareness. A developmental stage defines your level of maturity.

A state of mind is temporary, but states are integrated into your stage of development. If your developmental stage is still immature, you risk incorporating high spiritual views into childish behavior. So you can accept your state of mind, while working to improve your developmental stage.

This means developing the capacity to stay in relationship to physical sensations whenever threat arises. It's counterintuitive to stay with, for example, your panic or anxiety. It's a discipline that takes practice. You don't need to immediately react to perceived threats. You can learn to tolerate them in the body. This is the edge we walk when bringing practice to life circumstances.

If you want to improve your skills, you must first establish a friendly relationship with where you are. Start where you are. It's like a map: unless you know your location on the map, it's useless. Accept your experience while acknowledging the possibility of improvement.

So in order to effectuate change, we have to first accept the situation as is. It's pointless to push against the norm—as egregious as it may be—without first doing your own work of tolerating what is. You can't pass off your burdens to someone else.

Freedom

When you can accept whatever arises without struggle, you are approaching freedom. Freedom is an attitude—a way of experiencing things, not a fixed state of mind to achieve.

This is not to say that you won't have preferences—I will always choose raspberries over durian—but that you are capable of being content whether your wishes are met or unmet.

Rather than working to improve your experience, you can practice accepting things exactly as they are. It doesn't mean you will always like it. You may hate it.

Acceptance means acknowledging and allowing, at least for a moment, that things are just as they are, like it or not. Freedom is conscious participation in this experience of open awareness and acceptance.

THEN, and only then, you can discover the cracks in the system.

Writing Practice: Accepting What Is

Answer the following questions, using the free writing technique. Spend fifteen to thirty minutes with each question.

- What situation or event in your life has been the most challenging to accept?
- What would it take for you to unconditionally accept your situation as it is right now, without getting what you want, or getting rid of what you don't want?
- How could you give yourself permission to be who you are, just as you are, right now?
- How can you accept the unacceptable?

13

Signs of Progress

Cosmic Testing

After being with me one whole night
You ask how I live when you're not here.
Badly, frantically, like a fish trying to breathe
Dry sand.
You weep and say,
But you choose that.

—Rumi

Here's a fun feature of the journey: you must prove beyond a shadow of a doubt that you have learned your lesson. That you have been truly transformed. Be assured: the universe will test you. Again and again and again.

Until you pass.

Joseph Campbell even identifies this as one of the stages of the hero's journey. Once the villain has been conquered, the protagonist must battle or escape again, or learn to stand her ground.

I had not learned to stand my ground. And my faith was unraveling.

For years I'd prayed for a hand to hold, someone to love and to love me back. Now, once I stopped praying, let it all go to hibernate in a dilapidated shack in Bhutan intent on meditating away the rest of my days, then he came—my man in shining armor. I met him in the United States while I was still living in Bhutan. He rocked my world.

So I doubted the situation. None of it made any sense. I didn't know if my doubts were founded upon wisdom, or if they were simply manifestations of my own confused psychology. All the spiritual practice in the world will not heal a broken psychology.

I didn't trust my intuition.

I still told myself I needed a relationship, even though my recent experiences had shown me I could find happiness without one. I was happy as a yak in Bhutan, living my simple life in rustic surroundings, connecting more and more deeply to practice, and by extension, creativity. The more I streamlined my life to include serious doses of meditation retreat, the happier I became. I loved my exotic, nomadic life.

Yet the idea of fitting in, of living a traditional life with the respect and social standing I might earn from that, ("Thank God, my daughter has finally settled down") was a powerful pull. I wanted so badly to have a stable relationship. I was blind, grasping at justifications. In complete denial.

One afternoon, by chance, the state oracle for the Bhutanese royal family happened to be at the hotel. I knew her from Bodhgaya, where we had done prostrations next to each other. I asked her to perform a divination for me. I wanted her advice on whether or not to return to Colorado to spend the winter with the man I had been seeing.

We sat down in the lobby of the hotel and she took out a tiny bag filled with what appeared to be stones. She shook them like dice and rolled them three times, mumbling under her breath.

"What is your question?" she asked.

Her young assistant translated for us.

"I want to know whether I should go back to Colorado to spend time with this man or if I should stay here in Bhutan and continue practicing," I said.

She shook the stones and observed how they landed. She paused with eyes closed for a few minutes.

"If you stay here your practice will go extremely well. There will be no obstacles, and your work will go well too. Your practice will become very stable," she said.

"If you go back to see your friend, it will not be bad, but there will be many obstacles, and this will cause a lot of negativity."

I considered this.

One thing I had learned from the Vajrayana teachings was not to shy away from situations.

"Well, isn't part of practice also working with the level of samsara?" I asked her.

"Of course," she said, smiling. "It's up to you which practice you do—solitary retreat here in Bhutan, or worldly practice in the United States. Either way."

Though my heart was focused on practice, I wondered if staying in Bhutan was taking the easy route. Relationship was my most challenging life issue. If I really wanted to wake up, shouldn't I lean in? Don't they always say, "leap and the net will appear?"

Or rather, jump and break every bone in your body? And what self-respecting masochist wouldn't choose that option?

Like Naropa following his guru's instructions: Tilopa points and you jump. Why would you do this? Because to not jump is to ignore the call, refusing to grow.

Do I regret not taking the easy way out of that one? Sometimes. I loved my life in Bhutan. I've probably never felt so consistently peaceful and tuned-in as I did when I lived there. But there were also many obstacles.

In any case, I jumped. I broke every bone in my body. Why? Because in order to move through the karma that kept me stuck in that pattern, I had to live it out until it broke me.

You can't bypass the demon at the gate. The demons must be overcome, by force, cunning or coercion, but they must be dealt with.

What's your pattern? The one that keeps you awake at night, the one you think will ruin you if you give in to it.

Who is your demon? And what is your weapon?

The spiritual path is just that: a path. It's not a destination. Once you learn one lesson, there is another. You just keep on going forward, jumping when prompted. Do your practice and all is coming.

Revisioning Failure

Perhaps failure is the medicine we all need to recognize this giant truth, the one no one wants to discuss. Failure is an arbitrary concept. Ultimately, there is nothing to achieve, no goal, no "right way." Viewed from that perspective, there is no such thing as failure.

How can you fail if there's nothing to achieve?

This path we call spiritual is not about sailing through a clear sky toward a multicolored ray of blinding light.

These memories that make up a life, from the biggest mistakes to the smallest hurts, and all the good times in between, these are the material you have to work with, the proverbial grist for the mill.

If you can't identify and speak about your suffering, there's no way you will be able to transcend it.

So your stories, as embarrassing as they may be to expose, are what make up a life—in this case, your life.

The big lesson is that it is all an illusion, created as a game, created for us—and by us—to learn to love each other, and ourselves.

When you can love it all, you are home free.

After over twenty-five years of devoted—bordering on obsessive—yoga and meditation practice, I was amazed at how much time I still spent criticizing myself, judging others and wanting things to be different than they are. Wanting things, in general. Or not wanting things. Mad at how our planet was evolving. I used to hear stories about long-time practitioners who suddenly gave up practice after years and years, and I couldn't understand how anyone could be so silly. How could you give up after putting so much time in?

I got it. What did I really have to show for all the months and months on retreat, attending hundreds of teachings, classes and conferences? I'd spent thousands of dollars and many years, cumulatively, in intensive practice situations. I'd sacrificed steady jobs, long-term relationships, stable housing situations.

Good old ego kept asking: *Why are you wasting your time?*

I answered with things like this: *These practices settle me, I'm more stable emotionally, they have allowed me to earn my living while helping people and traveling the world, often in places most people only dream about. I spend entire days dwelling in peaceful bliss. It's been an incredibly rich experience.*

Or more to the point: *I don't have a choice.*

Ego answered: *You're a failure at this. Give it up.*

And of course this was true. I was a failure at it because there was nothing to achieve. There is no goal. And ego hates this. But along the way I had become more peaceful, more relaxed, nicer to be around. People told me so. This is the point of these practices. But you can't really measure that. And how do you list that on your resumé?

Yoga and meditation practice won't make life less intense. On the contrary, they sometimes even make things more intense, but they also teach you how to tune your system so that it is more capable of tolerating the voltage of that intensity.

I understood the point of practice to be a realization of the nature of mind—a realization that fundamentally shifts your perspective of reality. One that allows loving-kindness, compassion, joy, and equanimity to infiltrate every situation that arises. And though these qualities were more familiar than they had been in the past, for the most part, often, I still looked at the world in the same old way: through the eyes of ego, which asked in an endless variety of ways: *What's in it for me?*

Ego constantly complains. Things are never as we think they should be. We want more of this and less of that; we want to be somewhere else on the spectrum. But we're not. We're right exactly where we are.

I had to go back to the beginning. Being a beginner is humbling. Humility can be a profound teacher, if you are brave enough to face it.

Here is the beginner's practice: breathe in, breathe out. Smile. Repeat. It's also the advanced practice.

Psychological Maturity

Pilgrimage is essentially about growing up. Somewhere along the way you learn that a belief you held is untrue. Disillusionment sets in and you replace the false belief with a truth.

Isn't that what growing up is all about?

Maturing is learning to tolerate the challenges of life. Lack of adult capacities results in anxiety—all the emotional upheavals that accompany it. Drama.

Conversely, anxiety can interfere with ability to exhibit adult capacities. So if you want to learn to manage your mind, you need to become an adult.

What does that mean?

A few features are: delayed gratification, empathy for others, and the ability to take responsibility for yourself and your emotions. Bruce Tift's book, *Already Free*, is an excellent resource for this journey.

You are not alone in your pain on the path. That pain is part of the path—you're not doing it wrong because it hurts. This is essentially the point of pilgrimage: to know that it's okay—required— to confront your pain. It's part of the process of growing up. It's taking personal responsibility.

The problem is that most people equate growing up with conforming to the expectations of some society or system. But maturity from a spiritual perspective means thinking for yourself, and taking responsibility for your beliefs. It's about transforming an inherited naive worldview into discriminating wisdom.

The journey mirrors the internal transformation, and the new outer landscapes find parallels in the inner landscape. Outer signs, as exciting and reinforcing as they may be, are not as important as inner transformation.

The whole point of pilgrimage is to change your mind—to change the way you experience being alive.

One of Tibet's great saints said, "The best signs of success [in practice] are a decrease in self-centeredness and an easing of mental afflictions."

Essentially there is no path other than a commitment to live with authenticity and integrity in each present moment. Then you realize that even though you might feel alone, you are not alone.

Trust your inner wisdom and develop a relationship with that— even in the face of opposition. Because opposition may be afraid of disrupting status quo. I might even say that wisdom is disrupting your own status quo.

Writing Practice: Revisioning Failure

Where have you suffered most, or failed more miserably than all others? This is where the door to your heart is. A broken heart is an open heart.

Write for twenty minutes, answering this question:

- What has been your biggest failure?

Then do another twenty minute free writing session, answering this question:

- What is your expertise? Where have you earned your ten thousand hours? That's what you are an expert at.

Now do another writing session, free-associating the relationship between these two aspects.

- How does your failure inform your expertise? (For example, does your illness inform your art? Is your athleticism the result of feeling bullied as a child? Is your vivid imagination the result of chronic loneliness?)
- What is the relationship between your perceived failures and your gift?
- How can your expertise inform your suffering so that you can help others who suffer the same predicament?
- How can your suffering inform your expertise so that your gifts can be brought forth into the world to shine?
- What's your pattern? The one that keeps you awake at night, the one you think will ruin you if you give in to it?
- Who is your demon?
- What is your weapon?

14

Bringing Practice to Daily Life

~~~

Finding Sacred in Every Day

You can find sacred in every moment of life if you are open to it. This is the practice—opening yourself to life. To others. To experience. To all that you might not want to confront.

This is where the transformation happens—not on a mountaintop in Nepal or Tibet, or a retreat cabin in the silent dark woods, but in your heart. You can go there anytime, free of charge, instantly. No ticket needed.

You don't need a priest or a prophet or a rabbi or an imam.

Teachers can help. They can point you in the right direction, give you practices to help you steer, show you when you've gone off-track. But a spiritual path is different from following a religion.

But if you are not willing to feel your pain, to open yourself to the experience of being alive, experiences that you may not always understand, or like, unless you are willing to open yourself to what you may have spent a lifetime trying to avoid, then nobody—not Buddha, not Jesus, not Mother Mary herself—can make you have that experience.

It's up to you. Your life is a pilgrimage. Find the path quality as it makes sense to you.

The ongoing, daily practice is to recognize the nature of your mind, and then rest in the awareness of that.

Protecting the Mind

Vajrayana Buddhism is sometimes called the secret mantra path. A mantra is a seed syllable or phrase that you chant either aloud or silently. Mantras are said to protect the mind from disturbing emotions and discursive thinking. It's a tool to keep you in the present moment.

Om is a seed syllable.
Om mani padma hum is a seed phrase.

Thrangu Rinpoche writes: "Protecting mind from the disturbing emotions and discursive thought can be compared to protecting oneself from thieves. Thieves will know not to attack a strong, powerful, well-disciplined and attentive person. Rather they will attack someone who is sloppy and lazy and weak. Mindfulness and awareness make one strong, attentive, and well-disciplined. With these one cannot be robbed by disturbing emotions and discursive thought. Someone who lacks mindfulness and awareness is the one who will be plundered. What is stolen are the roots of beneficial factors that exist within one's mind. With mindfulness and awareness, the disturbing emotions will have no hope of being able to rob you and will just give up."

Next time you find yourself dwelling in negativity or fired up with anger, try silently reciting a mantra and notice what changes.

Four Immeasurables

Both Hindu and Buddhist views recognize the Four Immeasurables, or Brahma Viharas, as foundational cornerstones of emotional stability. These are heart-centered practices that help you work with emotions, and are designed to help shift perspective from a "me"-centered reality into an open attitude of acceptance.

The Four Immeasurables (with Sanskrit names) are:

- Loving-kindness, Maitri
- Compassion, Karuna
- Empathetic Joy, Mudita
- Equanimity, Upeksha

When you engage these practices to develop loving-kindness, compassion, empathetic joy, and equanimity, you essentially train the heart and mind to be happy. Each of these qualities counteracts negative emotions that conspire to make us suffer from hatred, passion, jealousy, and arrogance.

What makes the qualities immeasurable is that you extend them to everyone.

They also offer a handy template for living your life.

Loving-kindness

Indian rickshaw drivers often decorate their vehicles in outrageous fashion—glitter tassels, sparkly OM decals, plastic statues of Hanuman and baby Krishna bouncing on the dashboard as the woofer (taking up the whole trunk) blares Bollywood favorites directly into the passenger's eardrums.

More often than not (it seems) there is a life-size poster taped up in the back seat of a mother holding a newborn, gazing lovingly into its eyes. A mother's love, in its purest form.

Unconditional love. It always reminds me of the first immeasurable: maitri, or loving-kindness.

Loving-kindness is the simple aspiration to be happy. This includes wishing for your own happiness as well as the happiness of all beings. True happiness—not temporary happiness.

But it's more than a wish—it is the confidence that you can actually be happy—that you deserve to be happy—and it involves an active participation in that process.

True happiness is not dependent on outer circumstances; it comes from within. You must learn to recognize true happiness before you can aspire to it. That recognition of what makes you truly happy is called developing loving-kindness.

Of all the skills you will learn in life, perhaps the most important one is to develop loving-kindness. When you can extend loving-kindness to yourself then you can extend it to others.

I sometimes coteach a program for graduate psychology students with Naropa University. We head up into the mountains to meditate and go off-grid for two weeks. The theme of these retreats is Maitri Space Awareness practice, a unique approach to working with emotions developed by Chögyam Trungpa Rinpoche.

The practice is to evoke various emotional tones so that students get to experience their unique response to various emotions. How do you work with anger, or jealousy, or passion? What we inevitably discover is that the open space of loving-kindness can hold anything. Emotional challenges can be managed by offering loving-kindness and space to everything that arises.

What inhibits loving-kindness? Essentially, whenever you judge or compare yourself to others, you inhibit loving-kindness. When you solidify into a fixed point of view, you prevent the space that would otherwise hold a situation and allow it to breathe.

You have access to news feeds anytime you want. All this noise can wreak havoc on your state of mind. It induces fear, anger, hope, insecurity, jealousy, comparison, competition, and judgment.

Pressure to fit in, look a certain way, or accomplish goals can make you feel like you fall short. It takes heroic discipline to avoid getting hooked.

How do you avoid getting hooked? By recognizing that you are whole and complete just as you are, right here and right now. By developing loving-kindness.

Make a habit—a practice—of returning to awareness in the present moment without elaboration. When you can give yourself a break for not being perfect, you are on your way to the experience of loving-kindness.

When you are able to give space, you invite the possibility of acceptance, which is the ultimate act of love. The way to develop loving-kindness is to give space to situations and accept things exactly as they are, flaws and all.

You don't have to immediately rush to fix a problem, or react to a strong emotion. When you notice that you are being hard on yourself, take a mental step back and let the situation or circumstances breathe. Let things be messy for a moment. Giving things space allows for new perspectives to arise. Then you realize that your happiness is not dependent on outside circumstances.

Sometimes it seems easier to be kind to others than it is to be kind to ourselves. If this is true for you, try looking at yourself through the eyes of someone who loves you, and see what they see.

A Practice to Develop Loving-kindness

Years ago while on a retreat at Wat Suon Mok in Thailand, I learned a wonderful mantra that helps remind me to return to loving-kindness when I start getting hard on myself.

I offer it here in case it might help you remember that you are perfect just as you are, and exactly where you are meant to be:

May I be happy,
May I be well,
May I let go of the past.

You can also make this aspiration for others:

May you be happy,
May you be well,
May you let go of the past.

Try reciting this while sitting in traffic next to a homeless person, or standing in the queue at the pharmacy with sick people. Practice it for the sad-looking cashier at the 7-Eleven. You will be amazed at the difference it can make.

Watch how your attitude shifts when you keep loving-kindness in your heart as you go about your day.

Compassion

As the Dalai Lama notes, "If you want others to be happy, practice compassion; if you want to be happy, practice compassion."

Compassion means to suffer with. *Passion* from the past participle stem of Latin *pati* means "to suffer, endure," and *com* means "with" or "together."

When you put others' well-being before your own, you bypass the egoic stance of holding on tightly to your own experience and trying to get what will benefit only you.

Ironically, releasing this grip is what brings about true happiness.

Because here's the thing: impermanence is a fundamental truth. You can't hold on to anything. Once you realize that your experience is constantly in flux, wishing for the well-being of others is the only true way to subvert the system.

Ordinary compassion is the simple wish for others to be free of suffering. You probably feel it when you see an animal hurt on the side of the road. It is natural to feel for any being who is suffering, if you are paying attention. Developing compassion is a practice of evoking this mental muscle on a regular basis, through wishing others well. Immeasurable compassion is extending this wish to all beings, regardless of your feelings toward them.

When I was at my most hopeless phase—right around the time I turned forty—I finally discovered a glimmer of compassion. For myself. It was the only thing that kept me going for a while.

The shame I felt for having been single my entire life was overwhelming. And I kept choosing very sexy men who would love me and leave me, often in brutally abrupt ways. They were not all like that, but there were enough of them to leave a mark.

I was on retreat somewhere—probably Vietnam, where I often went to find sanctuary from Hong Kong—and my heart was breaking. The man I loved was with another woman.

I had learned a compassion meditation early on while I was at Naropa, but had never really done it faithfully. But I was desperate for some relief, so I tried it. Breathe in the suffering of the world, breathe out goodness and light.

Suddenly all the heartache I felt was absorbed into the totality of the world's suffering, and my heart broke open. I felt the pain that "the other woman" would soon enough feel (when he left her, too, which he did) and it was ironically this compassion for the other woman that broke my own spell. I stepped outside of myself long enough to see that my own suffering was just part of life; something we all experience. If I extend compassion to others, then I can also offer it to myself.

That was a big turning point for me. So I always recommend the sending and taking—tonglen—practice as a staple in your toolbox of practices.

Developing immeasurable compassion means making the aspiration that all beings may be free of suffering, not just the people in your small circle of loved ones. This means extending out your compassion to limitless beings throughout time and space, including Hitler, Osama bin Laden, the Shoe Bomber, and your ex-husband. Be thankful you have one.

And yes, even him.

This is no easy task at the beginning. It is easier to start developing immeasurable compassion with beings who you can relate to—and care about. Your cat, for example, or your favorite grandparent. Start with them and develop the practice slowly.

It can help to remember that everyone was a small child once, and had a mother who loved them, if even only for a moment. Every sentient being wants to be happy. Some just get more misguided about it than others.

Empathetic Joy

True joy comes from wishing others well. Empathetic joy is a wholesome attitude of rejoicing in the happiness and virtues of all sentient beings. This type of joy is different from worldly happiness in that you may not feel especially cheerful. It's more like a feeling of being content. It is the absence of struggle.

You know the feeling of joy when a close friend or family member encounters good fortune? This is the flavor of the third immeasurable. You learn to be happy because others are. But you don't just stop at your friends and loved ones.

Practicing empathetic joy means you take delight in sharing it with others. You recognize that joy cannot be hoarded, divided up, or stolen. Joy gets bigger when you share it. This is what gives it the "immeasurable" quality.

When you extend empathetic joy to all sentient beings, you experience true joy as a sublime state of mind. It is the perfect antidote to jealousy and envy and comparison.

It means relishing the good you see in the world, both in yourself and others. You feel happy when good fortune is bestowed on others.

You see that this life is fleeting and ephemeral, and that you could actually appreciate your life more because of this. Eventually you will have to let go of everything. Why not focus on the simple joys of living in the present moment?

Joy is really just about feeling okay with how things are.

Equanimity

Equanimity is an attitude of radical acceptance. It is regarding all sentient beings as equals. It is viewing all apparent phenomena as dreamlike, illusory, and impermanent.

When you recognize all that arises as temporary, you can accept whatever arises, whether or not the situation conforms to your wishes. Everything changes, so it's pointless to get worked up about something that will eventually evolve or dissolve.

Without an attitude of equanimity, failure is virtually synonymous with suffering. But with equanimity, failure is simply a big cosmic NO, directing you to something more suitable.

Mental steadiness and emotional balance in the face of change are your best defenses against suffering. You don't let things get to you. You learn to tolerate experience. That's called cultivating equanimity.

To become a sublime state of mind—an immeasurable—you extend this attitude of equanimity to all sentient beings. You recognize that all beings suffer. Equanimity allows you to be more tolerant of others when they act out of suffering.

You can see how easy it is for your relationships to transform: a friend becomes an enemy, a lover becomes a stranger, an enemy becomes a family member. These relationships may transform yet again.

When you develop immeasurable equanimity, you see that everyone—whether friend, lover, enemy, frenemy, or stranger—is, underneath it all, simply a sentient being struggling to find happiness.

A Different Take: Brahma Viharas

My dear Acharya Shankaranarayana once gave an interesting teaching in Mysore on these four brahma viharas from a Hindu perspective. He often taught that one of the most important ways of strengthening your practice was to choose carefully who you spend time with. The theme of resonance works in the opposite direction as well—you adopt habits from people in your circles. So if all your friends are yoga practitioners, chances are you will start practicing yoga. If you mix with drug dealers, you will learn tricks of the trade—a well-known phenomenon in the prison industry.

When you encounter people in your life, according to this interpretation of the brahma viharas, you extend to them what is appropriate to the situation. To someone who is a good influence you extend loving-kindness. For people who are kind-hearted but destructive, you extend compassion. Extend empathetic joy to someone who has questionable motives, but is basically harmless—a corrupt businessperson, for example. And for someone who is most difficult, someone whose behavior causes harm, you extend equanimity.

Ideally, the hope is to extend all four of these qualities to all beings. But in reality, if you are not able to extend loving-kindness to someone, then try compassion. If that's not possible, go for joyful empathy. If that doesn't work, then at least try to be equanimous and let it go.

I've never heard this particular slant taught in Buddhist teachings, and I only heard it once from Acharya. But I found it helpful as a practical way to apply the four immeasurable qualities.

Practice in Daily Life

Bringing practice to daily life is about turning every day into a pilgrimage, and that requires a shift in attitude. We bring our practice into the world to be of benefit to our ailing planet and its inhabitants. Here's the irony: the practice is simply learning to take care of yourself.

When you take care of yourself, you model for others how to live sanely, with simplicity.

The first step in knowing how to take care of yourself is to learn to identify when you start going off track. The body will tell you this information if you listen. But it's like learning a new language for many of us who have spent years ignoring the messages our bodies are telling us.

Here are twelve ways to take care of yourself:

1. **Learn to listen to your body.** This is much different than the idea of listening to your body. This is why yoga is such a powerful tool—it gets us in the body on a deep level so we can start to be aware of the messages our bodies give us. The body does not lie—and it will speak up in its own language when we need to pay attention to something. Place your hand too close to the fire and you will get an immediate—and loud—message. Some

messages are more subtle and harder to read. The more
in tune we are with our physical body, the easier it
becomes to read these signs.

2. **Eat what nourishes you.** So much of what gets sold
   as food these days is not even food! You don't have
   to get neurotic or rigid about it, but research clearly
   shows that eating well is our best defense against illness.
   Go for fresh, locally sourced produce grown without
   pesticides or chemicals, reduce sugar and unhealthy
   cooking oils, avoid MSG and foods that contain
   preservatives. It's pretty simple. Just eat good food! I
   have a general rule of thumb that if it comes out of a
   box, I don't eat it. If cooking healthy food seems too
   overwhelming, learn a few simple dishes that you can
   keep as fallbacks to make it easy to succeed. If you don't
   have a backup plan, it can be too easy to go for fast
   food, which is usually not the best way to nourish your
   body. Taking care of yourself means planning ahead.

3. **Clean up your environment.** Are you living in a
   toxic environment? Toxicity can take many forms:
   environmental toxins can be obvious as in air pollution,
   or subtle, like when you discover you have mold infesting
   your walls. There are toxic relationships and communities,
   and we can speak to ourselves in toxic ways. We ingest
   toxins when we don't pay attention to what we eat, or
   consciously when we indulge in drugs or alcohol. This
   is usually a simple fix, but the hard part comes in our
   attachment to habitual patterns. Taking care of yourself
   means eliminating or reducing toxins from your body,
   environment, relationships, and emotional state.

4. **Get regular exercise.** There are so many studies linking good health to regular exercise that most of us are pretty aware we need to move regularly if we want to practice self-care. Just get in a routine that feels manageable—not too hard, not too soft—and stick with it. Bonus points if you get outdoors to reconnect with nature as you exercise.

5. **Prioritize sleep.** This is such an easy and quick way to introduce self-care on a profound level. It's amazing more of us don't do this. Notice I didn't say: get enough sleep. Most of us can function on less-than-optimal sleep, and convince ourselves that we are getting enough shut-eye. But to prioritize sleep, we start looking at all the ways we sabotage our rest cycle through stimulants, computer screens late at night, unresolved emotional issues, taking on too much, and generally not being aware of our natural rhythms. Try a phase of making sleep your #1 priority and see how your attitude shifts.

6. **Develop nourishing relationships and set boundaries with unhealthy ones.** We pick up habits from the people we spend time with. It is important to carefully choose the people you spend the most time with. If you hang out with a gang, you'll eventually become a gangster. If you hang out with kind, compassionate people, you'll become one of them.

7. **Speak kindly, especially to yourself.** Speak kind, truthful words, and notice how your mind-set changes. Most of us spend a lot of time criticizing or judging our experience. Even the smallest incident can bring on a

wave of negativity: you're trying to get a new app to work on your phone and it is not cooperating so you swear at the damn thing (see?). Watch how you do this...the way we use speech creates energy patterns that infuse the body and send out signals into the environment. If you are constantly lashing out in criticism—even if it is only in your mind—you are germinating a toxic inner environment. Antidote: Breathe and smile. Or...

8. **Chant an affirming mantra, out loud or silently.**
    - May I be well, May I be happy, May I let go of the past
    - Om mani padme hum
    - Or hum a song—it's surprising how calming this is.

9. **Manage stressors.** Learn to say no. This benign little word can be very empowering. Get clear on what supports your well-being and what stresses you out. You might want to add "thank you."

10. **Meditate daily.** A daily meditation practice will do more for your self-care than most anything else. When you take time each day to check in with yourself, you start to notice patterns. We can only change what we are aware of.

11. **Practice gratitude.** Make a practice of recognizing the kindness others extend to you and share your appreciation with them. When you focus on positive qualities guess what you attract more of?

12. **Breathe.** Whenever you think of it, notice your breathing. It's the most reliable way to quickly change

your state of mind. If you find yourself getting worked
up about something, take a few deep breaths, and
observe the shift.

Writing Practice: Living with Intention

For each of the following, write about a situation that either evokes
or needs one of the four immeasurables.

Loving-kindness

- ᔕ What would you love to receive?
- ᔕ How can you be more kind to yourself?
- ᔕ Where does your heart call you to go?

Compassion

- ᔕ What causes you to suffer?
- ᔕ How can you offer compassion to yourself and others?
- ᔕ What would compassion for yourself look like?
- ᔕ To discover this, listen to a guided meditation I've
  prepared for you in the Resources section.

Empathetic Joy

- ᔕ What makes you happy?
- ᔕ How is others' happiness related to your own?
- ᔕ Remember a time when you felt happy for someone's
  success and write about how you felt.

Equanimity

- ᔕ What causes you to feel off-center?
- ᔕ When have you felt unflappable?
- ᔕ Where can you create more balance

15

Change of Heart

Trust Yourself

At a certain point you have to stop looking to others to give you answers and listen to your inner guide. That doesn't necessarily mean leaving your teachers behind (although it can). It means shifting your allegiance to the source of wisdom, rather than relying on an intermediary. Once you have the practices, you just have to do them. Every damn day.

Developing a daily practice is not a linear event. But when you discipline yourself to sit down every day and give space to your experience, the chatter settles down so that eventually you can sift through and find the nuggets of wisdom.

These are the choices you have to make as you negotiate your path. No one can make them for you. This is why pilgrimage is so potent—it puts you in situations where you must decide for yourself how to proceed.

When you embark on pilgrimage, you set out on an adventure that's not about following your ego's whims (chasing fame, fortune, desire) or the cookie cutter dreams made for you by people too afraid to step outside their own boxes, by a world dedicated to keeping you in line with their values.

It's not about "deciding" where to go, which route to follow. Learn to listen to, then hear your inner guidance. It means tuning in to your intuition—something you might not usually be encouraged to do. Listen for what feels right. Learn to read the signs. You know. But you've probably been trained to ignore.

Most of us have been trained from birth to mistrust the voice of our intuition. Stop ignoring the voice of wisdom that speaks to and through you every day of your life.

Trust it. Trust yourself. Wait for the call, the sign, the urge to act. Then go.

Daily Practice

Throughout this book I've frequently referred to this idea of practice. What is a practice? Doctors, lawyers, and psychotherapists have practices where they deliver their professional services. Musicians and athletes practice to hone their skills. You can practice moves for a dance routine or technical skills for a creative endeavor.

So what does it mean to have a "yoga practice"? When do you shift from dabbling in meditation to having a "meditation practice"?

The turning point for me came that day I made myself turn around and sit down on my cushion as I was walking out the door. There was a shift that happened when I realized how important it was for me to meditate every day. I committed.

Prior to that I had already committed to my yoga practice, though that felt less like a commitment than an obsession. There was just no choice in the matter. It was what I did. I went to the yoga studio to practice every day.

Even if there are days or phases now when I am lazy or half-hearted, there is no longer any doubt about my commitment. I know it's just a matter of time before I return to the cushion.

The same goes for my yoga practice. This is a bit more complex, as my practice has evolved so dramatically over the years—as will yours. When people ask me these days whether I still practice Ashtanga Vinyasa Yoga, I say, "It depends who's asking." I no longer do a full intermediate or advanced series practice as I used to do six days a week. Thanks to age and injury, those days are gone! But I do practice an abbreviated version of the primary series, with ujayi pranayama, dristi, and bandhas, most days. And this is still more than I was doing at the beginning of my yoga journey, before I even knew about the Ashtanga series.

My point is that a practice relies less on the actual details of the ritual, and more on the intention. When you make it a priority in your life, practice will evolve in surprising and often magical ways. It's as if you set a daily date with the divine. If you keep showing up, something or someone else will meet you there.

Your way of coming about it will be different from mine, or anyone else's. Some people develop a practice because they connect so strongly with a teacher. Some are magnetized toward a particular practice. Often circumstance plays a role: it depends on the resources that are available in your locale. Others may be attracted to a community that practices together. This last doorway can be a nice way to get support as you develop your own practice.

But be clear that the doorway is not all that important. The entry into practice is just that. Once you're in, you get to explore the whole house, and if you choose to move in, you can settle into one room for the rest of your life if you wish. After all, the essence of an authentic practice is developing a relationship to your Self, with a big *S*. Your lineage might name it something different, but essentially that's what we are doing.

You don't have to do a fancy practice. It can be as simple as sitting quietly to follow your breath five minutes a day. What makes it a practice is that you give it priority.

Not Expecting Results

You might think that by practicing deep meditation and yoga that you can avoid the work, and the pain of life, but in fact the opposite is true. Deep practice invites suffering, because this is how you burn off karma.

Chögyam Trungpa Rinpoche was so clear on this point—that the meditation is simply the way in—a way to start developing a sane relationship to your present experience and that, if anything, it would most likely make life more intense, excruciating, and miserable at times.

Despite deep practice and devotion, still the world turns round and round, still there is suffering. When everything falls apart, moments of quiet contemplation reconnect you to the earth, and to your wounded heart.

"It's not about happiness," Chögyam Trungpa Rinpoche said. "It's about something much more interesting than that."

But how do you get any relief from that kind of statement? Is there any relief? Some sort of cosmic painkiller?

There is, my friend. It's called love. I know; you've heard it before.

The love I'm talking about is not the special sauce—not the fairy-tale love of the cinemas. It's the love of things as they are—exactly as they are—right now. Because they can be no different. Rather than assuming you understand what is happening right now, just take a moment to listen. There is a stillness that comes from that listening, and that stillness is peace. It comes down to simply accepting what fate has tossed your way, accepting the pain and loss, the disappointment and letting that pierce to the core of your heart. Because a devastated heart is an open heart. Like Rumi says,

God's treasures lie in ruined hearts.

It is about learning to tolerate that experience—tuning in deeply enough so that intense pain becomes simply a deeper resonance, a different vibration on the musical scale and to learn to appreciate that sort of music. I don't say "like": you don't have to like it. But appreciate it, and accept it. Then you can love it.

Acceptance doesn't mean sitting by idly while people suffer—please, help our ailing planet. Love your Mother Earth. Protect her forests, aid her residents, honor the life-giving gifts she offers. Respect her. Serve her. She is sick and needs our care.

But before you can be of benefit—to others or yourself—you first have to accept the situation as it is. Then, and only then, can you act with wisdom. Wisdom is learning to tolerate experience by seeing that it is all an illusion, a game created for us to learn our lessons.

When you accept whatever you see and hear, not just with your eyes and ears, but with your whole body, then that is love. You can feel the love that is around you all the time. That love permeates every cell of your being. That is the secret. You don't need anyone to love. You just love what is—love it all. Start with yourself.

Learning to Love Yourself

Self-love comes to some of us not automatically, but rather by conscious effort. Whenever we compare ourselves to others, we inhibit love. Pressure to fit in, to look a certain way, or accomplish goals can make us feel like we fall short.

Often, that pressure is our own state of mind responding to the "outside" world's values. Our family, work environment, friends, and culture all influence us, whether consciously or unconsciously, to behave in certain ways. When we deviate from the established norm, we may criticize ourselves harshly for not measuring up.

For example, it's easy to get seduced by images of happy lives we see on social media, and hold ourselves to unrealistic ideals. All that personal PR can wreak havoc on our state of mind. We may feel everyone else has it all together, while we struggle with our fear, anger, and confusion. If we then add another layer of judgment, we've got a perfect recipe for self-criticism. Getting caught up in the carefully composed images of others' lives takes us out of the present moment. It takes heroic discipline to avoid getting hooked.

Self-love comes from giving space to situations and accepting things exactly as they are, flaws and all. When you notice that you are being hard on yourself, take a mental step back and let the situation or circumstances breathe. You don't have to immediately rush to fix a problem, or react to a strong emotion. Giving things space allows for new perspectives to arise. When you are able to give space, you invite the possibility of acceptance, which is the ultimate act of love. Then you realize that your happiness is not dependent on outside circumstances. That experience is pure freedom.

How Do You Learn to Love Yourself?

Recognize that you are whole and complete just as you are, right here and right now. Yes, that means even if there are things that feel out of alignment. We are perpetual works in progress—it is part of the human condition. The best way to start to silence the voice of your inner critic is to first learn to listen.

Make a habit—a practice—of returning to awareness in the present moment without elaboration. Just notice the urge to react, and step back to take in a larger vantage point. We learn to love ourselves by showing up for ourselves in times of need, rather than meting out punishment for not yet being perfect. When we allow ourselves to unfold in our own time, even if it is slower than what we want, or what others expect, we are practicing self-love.

When you can give yourself a break for not being perfect, you are on your way to developing self-love.

We all go through confusion at times in our lives. Recognizing this as part of the human process can take the pressure off so that we can show up for ourselves in times of need as a support, rather than as a critic.

How do you recognize self-love? Here are some ideas. You could come up with a few of your own.

- Taking care of yourself
- Being kind to others
- Respecting self and other
- Relaxed discipline
- Confident posture
- Doing what you know is in your best interest
- Ability to set boundaries
- Speaking up and using your voice

Transformation

How is transformation different from simple change? When you change your mind about something, it is reversible. You can always reverse your decision. Change is on the surface—you can change jobs or change boyfriends.

Transformation is a change of heart. There is no going back.

Like a caterpillar going into its cocoon, there is a sense of absolute disintegration. Restructuring occurs so that whoever emerges might bear no resemblance to your former self. There is a required period of not knowing; a complete releasing of the old self in order to prepare for the emergence of a new identity.

You might wonder: Am I saying you have to give up your old life?

Yes, that's what I'm saying. To be reborn, you must give up your old life. You might live in the same place with the same people, but your old way of seeing things will no longer be relevant.

Tools for Negotiating Transitions

Transition is an ongoing part of life. We are always in transition.

Here is a reliable truth: all things, eventually, fall apart. The Buddha's teachings advise that all composite things decompose. And everything is composite. Impermanence is just part of the plan.

The problem is not that things fall apart—that's just a law of nature. But you may experience this as a problem if your thoughts and emotions have not caught up with the reality. When things fall apart, it means change.

It's possible to learn to navigate change with grace with a few simple adjustments. Here are some of my favorite tools to help you negotiate life transitions.

1. **Relaxing is the key.** Transition means a disintegration of one set of circumstances in order to make room for another to arise. It can be scary. But unless you let go of what wants to pass, you won't be able to make room for new situations to arise.

   The key to successfully navigating a life transition is to relax. When you let go of your expectations and make friends with the situation, you invite curiosity. You become open to new perspectives that are coming into view. By allowing an attitude of relaxed openness, you open to new possibilities.

   I used to dread transitions and worried about things I could not foresee. Much of what is difficult about change is simply that there are unknowns. But when I learned to relax into change, I started to notice the feeling of excitement that accompanies transitions. From one perspective it may look like things are falling apart. From another, it is an opportunity, paving the way to a new phase of life. Transitions always offer the possibility of reinventing yourself.

2. **Accept things as they are.** You may dream of an ideal situation where things will go smoothly, forever— when you will be peaceful, happy, successful, and fulfilled. There are many people willing to help you do that: coaches, advisors, teachers, gurus, counselors, consultants. There's nothing wrong with learning skills to improve your circumstances. But the problem with this approach is relying exclusively on circumstances to make you happy. It's only a superficial, and temporary fix.

   More important than learning to manipulate your circumstances is learning to accept—and tolerate—what is happening in your current situation. Only from a place of acceptance can you eventually create change.

3. **Contemplation: Ground, Path, and Fruition.** Change means growth, if you pay attention. Think of it as evolution. It can be helpful to think of this as ground, path, and fruition. When you are confronting transition, contemplate (or better yet, do a free write for) these questions:

   Ground
   - What's happening right now? This could be as simple as describing your surroundings: sights, sounds, smells, and the surrounding situation.
   - What is your current reality?

- ෨ Are you happy with things as they are? Why or why not?

Path

- ෨ Where are you heading? If you were to take your hands off the steering wheel—metaphorically speaking—where would you end up?
- ෨ What is the trajectory in your life?
- ෨ Is it where you want to go?
- ෨ Could you avoid a collision by steering slightly or applying the brakes?

Fruition

- ෨ What are the possibilities from where you sit?
- ෨ What is your ideal outcome in the current situation?
- ෨ Do you have a vision of what that looks like?
- ෨ Can you identify supportive influences that are trying to help you progress along the right path?

4. **Write prompts for negotiating transitions.** One of the hardest parts about transitions is knowing which direction to take. Often the best advice comes from your inner wise guide who speaks through the written word. Use the following writing prompts:

- ෨ What's really bugging me right now...
- ෨ If I could say one thing to _____, I would tell them...
- ෨ To be honest, I would rather...
- ෨ I really need to let go of...
- ෨ What's happening right now is...

- ❧ I know when I'm really happy because...
- ❧ If I knew I could not fail, I would...
- ❧ The last time I felt this way, I...
- ❧ What I wish I could change is...
- ❧ What I need to accept is...
- ❧ How do I get in my own way?

Transitions are often accompanied by worry, stress, or anxiety. Tools such as these writing prompts help you gain perspective. Write until you feel a sense of clarity in your bones. If there's not a final solution that becomes clear, then do another free write, and go for small steps.

5. **Ask for guidance.** If nothing occurs to you through the contemplations or writing practices, then open yourself to grace. At times in my life when I've had no clear direction, I simply ask for clarity and guidance. Call it prayer if you will.

Settle in to your quiet place and ask. I often do this while walking in nature, or at the end of a meditation or yoga practice. Then make a practice of noticing signs in all forms: thoughts that arise, people or animals who cross your path (and the uncanny way strangers can give you messages when you least expect them), feelings, new situations that suddenly appear. It can be tempting to write off these "messages" as simply arbitrary coincidences, and wait for more glittery miracles. But the small miracles—in the form of these mundane messages—are often the signs pointing the way to move forward.

When you learn to trust the message of your inner wisdom—that often expresses itself through signs in the phenomenal world—you will have a new tool to help guide you through life transitions. The tricky part is to learn to quiet your mind enough to be able to hear these messages. So when transition is upon you, my best advice is to sit still and listen until you know what to do.

Writing Practice: Your Daily Self-Care Plan

Are you taking care of yourself? Sometimes it seems like we spend so much of our energy taking care of life's endless details that there's no time left to focus on our well-being. But I don't think it comes down to a lack of time. If we really want to make self-care a priority, we simply have to develop certain habits—and let go of habits that sabotage us.

Give yourself a good two hours to work on this one. It's a two-parter.

1. Free write answers to the following questions:

- When was the last time I trusted I was on the right path?
- What was I doing at that phase of my life that might have contributed to feeling good?
- What wasn't I doing at that phase of my life that might have contributed to feeling good?
- What has changed?
- What support do I want to receive?

2. Outline a sample list of daily activities that you'd like to adopt or recommit to. I like to use bullet lists for this type of thing.

16

Wisdom

Samsara or Nirvana?

The only difference between samsara and nirvana is your view of the phenomenal world. Grasping and revulsion perpetuate suffering. Wisdom means total acceptance of whatever arises, and letting go of any urge to try to fix things. From an ultimate perspective, good and bad are no different. There is only that which causes suffering, and that which heals it. Not everything can be fixed. I'm not saying don't support worthy causes. I'm saying don't fight things. Without acceptance, your actions will be based on aggression as you try to change the things that you can't accept.

Why is it so difficult to accept what is?

Failure, despair, loss, and rejection are hard pills to swallow. But why do we have this idea that we should be moving toward some goal? Where do we think we are headed? We get an idea about a result—how we want our life, our work, our relationships—to look, and then we get busy manipulating the phenomenal world to create that. And why not? Creation is an act worthy of the gods. But what happens when our masterpiece fails? What if we run out of paint? Lose our vision? What if it just doesn't work?

When you accept whatever it is that arises, not just with your mind, but with your whole being, then that is the beginning of wisdom.

Feminine Wisdom

Daily practice allows you to access your inner wisdom. It's checking in with HQ. A direct download.

Your practice connects you to the sacred feminine force.

Feminine wisdom does not teach by sitting at the head of a lineage or hierarchical system—it is more fluid than that. Feminine wisdom is shared by example: modeling and relating. Being with.

Established paths to religion often lead to wars. Even Buddhists have engaged in war (think Burma or Sri Lanka or early Tibet). The thing about following a religious tradition is that there is a power differential, and it's usually the men who hold the power. How often have we heard about men leading religious organizations who abuse their power?

To access wisdom, the only sane answer is to trust the intuitive power of the feminine—which is anathema to the patriarchy.

The spiritual path is about discovering your own source of wisdom—which is found in the natural world. It's about developing a relationship to the true source of your power, and living your life in harmony with it. My question is: What are we doing handing over our power to a religious institution—usually headed by a man—when we already have the power within us?

How can we give away our power and then expect to get it served back to us?

Teaching authorizations, certificates, degrees, lineages, permission, teacher trainings (as if you could teach someone to be a teacher...) are packages of the patriarchy, designed to categorize people among the ranks of hierarchy. I'm sure you know many wise people who have no paperwork to show. And I'm just as sure you know someone in a position of authority who acts like a complete idiot.

My sense is that it's up to us women to show the way—not by following a patriarchal religion—by learning to trust our inner wisdom as the guide. To collectively bring this wisdom into the light. That light belongs to everyone. It is our responsibility and gift to mentor and nurture each other as we make our way down this pathless path. I don't think it's an accident that this is exactly what we are confronting on the political stage at this juncture.

> If we continue to devalue what women have to
> offer, we will continue harming women and continue
> overlooking and devaluing these virtues that are
> considered "feminine" and these are precisely the
> virtues that the world needs most now.
> —His Holiness the 17th Karmapa, Ogyen Trinley Dorje

You have access to the universal energy, right in your own home. It's in your body. It's in nature. Your home is your body, in the natural world. In silence. You can access this energy through awareness.

When you hold your own power, you remember that you are part of the cycles of nature. You can ride the tsunami as it devastates the man-made structures. You can help the return to balance by nurturing this relationship to your sacred feminine fire.

In championing the sacred feminine, I'm not denying the importance of the masculine. I'm not man-bashing—and I'm eternally grateful to my male teachers and the supportive men in my life. Every human has both masculine and feminine energies—I don't think the answer is an "us" versus "them" debate.

It's simply that the feminine has been absent for too long. The scales have tipped too far into the domain of the masculine, and if you—man, woman, other—want to wake up to your inner wisdom, then you're going to have to acknowledge the mysterious wisdom of the feminine, grounded in the structure of the masculine.

We need both feminine and masculine. We need balance. Like light waves versus particles, we have to hold contradictory viewpoints simultaneously. A surfeit of masculine congeals into patriarchy. Who knows what an overabundance of feminine would create: equality and tolerance? A repeal of national borders? Respect for nature?

What if we created a harmonious union of the two?

Relax and Enjoy

My grandmother had a saying that I refer to regularly: relax and enjoy. Sometimes I think Toppy was a great yogini.

Eventually the practice takes you to a place where you have no further questions, because there are no relevant questions. Everything you can think of either has no answer, or you don't need to know the answer because when it is time, you will know. So you settle into a feeling of okayness, just being okay with what is.

Wisdom is natural. We are born with it. And then we cover it up with all sorts of stuff: hopes, expectations, thoughts, concepts, habitual patterns, judgment, criticism, speed, laziness, lack of self-care. We don't pay attention. The first step toward wisdom is paying attention.

At a certain point you'll start to realize that you have everything you need, for now. So the practice becomes resting in that now, again and again.

Rather than being constantly interrupted by instant messaging, you could set aside time every day to unplug and relax. By learning to rest and quiet the mind, you have choices about how and where to focus your awareness. You encourage resting in the present moment.

When you shift your mind-set to the present, you start to recognize new perspectives in the grand scheme of things. You can learn to ally with the spaciousness of the present moment instead of getting caught up in the stream of busyness. Yoga and meditation practice help this process. Done daily, you'll notice ongoing, cumulative results.

Routines

Living life as a pilgrim can be formless. Routines provide a structure to your day so that you don't get lost. At any given moment, you know what you are (or should be) doing. You're creating a container to hold your new identity and watch it evolve.

A container allows you to define the boundaries so your mind can relax and expand. When you lack a container, or when your container leaks, you lose the potency of all that practice you are doing. Establishing a daily routine allows a container for your mind to stay focused.

This is why retreat is such a powerful practice: you set aside time with no distractions to devote to recognizing your true nature. When you are out and about in your daily life, it is simply too distracting to delve into these deeper waters. You've got to keep your wits about you to avoid being hit by a truck, instead of settling into a state of spacious awareness that lies underneath the display of phenomena.

Another powerful way to establish a container for observing your evolution is to tap into the creative process. When you create regularly, you start to observe your own evolution: the ongoing process of being in the present moment. Once you start paying attention to this, you also start to see changes in your life. This will encourage you to grow in positive directions.

The point is to provide a structure from which to view the mind from the same perspective each day. The activity is the same, so the nuances of the mind reveal themselves. Creativity thrives in this environment. From my own experience, when you allow your creativity to have a voice, your own voice becomes more clear. You also start to hear it more loudly.

The Seed of Compassion

The Karmapa once said that true practice is to take on the suffering and pain of all beings, and to share your happiness with them as well. So suffering is the seed of compassion. Without the ability to contact and tolerate our own suffering, we cannot understand what others are going through.

By consciously taking on suffering—your own and others'—you expand the capacity of your heart. Ironically, this increases your capacity for joy, because your heart gets bigger. Then when you do have joy to share, it spreads infinitely larger.

The spaciousness of your mind and the depth of your heart have the capacity to hold anything. When something arises, you offer it back to the whole, to recycle. Suffering is suffering—there is no "yours" and "mine."

As soon as you acknowledge that simple fact, then it dissolves, and the thing that brought so much pain then becomes the letter of introduction, the initiation. The invitation to love.

Compassion: to suffer with.

When you sign up to take a deep look at things by practicing meditation in a disciplined way, you sign up for everything: good, bad, and ugly. Birth, old age, sickness, and death. There is no bypassing the latter two, no bargaining with Yama. The Lord of Death will have his way in the end. Things will come when they are good and ready, and they will fall apart just as easily, independent of your feelings about the whole phenomenal display. But good and bad ultimately are no different. In the end, it all evaporates like mist, revealing the beauty of simple suchness underneath.

The everyday practice then is to return to awareness and compassion as we make our way along the path.

Practice: Awareness of Awareness

Enlightenment—lightening up—occurs when you stop ignoring this wakeful mind. Meditation does not cause enlightenment—wakeful mind already exists.

Awareness is not dependent on external circumstances. You can be just as aware of a painful event as you can of a joyous occasion. The act of being aware is simply to take a step back from what you are aware of, and recognize the faculty of awareness.

Focus on something and then turn that awareness back on to itself.

Who or what is being aware?

Do this for just a short period—a minute or two—but regularly.

Try it throughout the day, in different circumstances, whenever you think of it.

Writing Practice: What Do I Know Is True?

This is a practice you can do forever. Adjust the details to apply to your current circumstances.

When you need guidance or support in making life decisions, you often have all the answers you need inside. Listen to the questions you are asking others and then pose them to yourself. Write the question at the top of a page and write. When you get stuck or lost, return to the question and start again. Keep going until you get an opening into a new line of thinking.

Afterword

Creative Process as Pilgrimage

I've heard it said that at the far reaches of science it becomes indistinguishable from magic. I've always felt that at the far reaches of spiritual practice comes art.

Like any discipline, spiritual or not, at a certain point you have to move on from practicing to the real performance—the creative expression that arises out of all that hard work. Why would you spend your whole life practicing something that never bears fruit? Or that you never had any fun with?

Creativity arises naturally when you stop striving to achieve something. There's a certain spontaneous appreciation of the world and a wish to play with those energies.

One of Chögyam Trungpa Rinpoche's gifts was a practice called "maitri space awareness." It's a playful approach to discovering how energies of the five elements manifest in different ways and how we personally respond to and re-create those energies in our lives.

> Water can manifest as peaceful calm or icy reflection.
> Earth can shower riches or become barren and dry.
> Fire manifests as passionate warmth or lusty destruction.
> Wind can clear away debris or create total chaos.
> Space can be accommodating or forgetful.

We are part of the natural world. When you start to know yourself and learn your habitual patterns of responding, you can bring new awareness to the process of living your life. The antidote to constricting energy is space. The antidote to fear is love.

I've discovered that the key to keeping this pilgrim state of mind is just a simple daily practice of yoga and meditation, daily walks outdoors, practicing self-love and generosity when I can. When things get tricky, space is usually a good answer.

More recently, practice includes a daily dose of painting. However your creativity shows up, let it lead you to your next adventure.

May your path be filled with peace, joy, inspiration, and ease.

Part 4

Resources

Introduction to Sitting Meditation

Shamatha meditation is a basic technique of taming and training the mind. Shamatha in Sanskrit means peace. With experience, this practice will show you how to make peace with your mind. That doesn't mean that you will always be peaceful. But you will discover how to cultivate this quality, and eventually to let it permeate your daily life more and more.

I recommend setting aside a separate time and space for the formal practice of sitting meditation. Early morning, evening around sunset, and just before bed are auspicious times. More important than how long you sit is how regularly. It is better to sit every day for five minutes than once a week for an hour. Even better is to sit every day for an hour. Regularity reinforces your commitment to yourself. It sends a message (that we may not even hear consciously at first) that you are serious about practice. This can have profound effects on your life.

The Posture

Sit on a cushion with the legs crossed, or sit with one foot in front of the other. It is important to sit comfortably straight, so that the mind is not preoccupied with physical pain. If your hips are very tight, sit up on a cushion high enough to allow the knees to be lower than the hips. It is useful to sit with the hips slightly elevated on a cushion in order to keep the circulation flowing. If necessary, you may sit in a chair with the feet flat on the floor, sitting up straight.

Place the hands down on the thighs at a distance that allows the shoulders to remain relaxed. Keep the eyes open. Let the shoulders settle directly above the hips. Sometimes it can be helpful to sway back and forth very slightly at first, to find, intuitively, that place that feels correct: where you are sitting tall and relaxed, and can easily breathe deeply. Often our habitual way of sitting is not aligned, and so when we do sit with alignment it feels strange or even unbalanced. Let the breath be your guide. It is easiest to take a deep breath when you are sitting in alignment.

Imagine that you are a flower growing out of the earth. Your roots grow deep down, anchoring you. The stalk, your spine, is firm and upright, and yet accommodates the subtle fluctuations that accompany growth and changes in the environment. The top of the head blossoms upward, as if drawn by the warmth of the sun.

The point of sitting in meditation is to allow the mind to rest, so if your body is screaming in pain, it will be difficult to settle the mind. Spend some time experimenting with different postures. Once you find one that works reasonably well, stick with it for a period of time. Try to resist the urge to move every time you feel discomfort. Discipline yourself, gently, to stay with that sensation. Allow the breath to soften whatever tightness or blockage you might notice. If you practice yoga asana, you will find that as you deepen the asana practice, your hips will loosen and allow you to settle more deeply into meditation posture. So there may be a process of evolution.

Follow the Breath

After you find a reasonably comfortable posture that encourages alertness, the instruction is to follow the breath with your awareness. Let the breath behave exactly as it wants to. Don't do anything at all to manipulate it. Just watch it very closely. In shamatha practice, you use the breath as a reference point, paying particular attention to the exhale. You can let the inhale happen on its own volition. This is the practice: to sit, patiently observing.

At the end of the exhale, notice the gap just before the inhale comes. Don't be in a hurry to move on to the next breath. Observe and appreciate the simple act of breathing. As you inhale, let your observation diffuse using a lighter touch. Don't necessarily try to follow the inhale, but rather let the mind rest, trusting that inhaling will happen without your intervention. Ride the next exhale with your awareness. Just learning to follow the breath is a feat in itself. I think it took me ten years of pretty intensive practice to actually pay attention to my first breath. So getting there is great news. Headline: Yogi Notices Breath for First Time.

You can observe the inhale and the exhale. However, if you choose this approach, then emphasize JUST slightly more the exhale. Exhale is release, giving up, surrendering. Inhale is taking in, holding on. Be bold: surrender.

Observing the Mind

You will probably notice that as you try to follow the breath, the mind wanders. Since you have not given it a specific task, other than to observe, mind has a tendency to get distracted. Observing is the hardest task of all, and the most important.

If you allow your mind to play itself out long enough, loudly enough, and keep coming back to the breath, eventually it will wear itself out. You train it like you would train a puppy, or teach a small child: consistently and gently. Keep showing the mind who is responsible by returning again and again to the breath. Not in an overly authoritarian way, but in a kind, knowing way. A wise way. Tell your mind, "I know all about you and your tricks. You try to dissuade me from paying attention to the breath. You are very clever. But I am wiser than you."

Notice where your mind goes. "Yes, I see that you are angry and are holding a grudge against your ex," tell it, "but now is not the time to do that. You can tell that person what you think later; now come back to the breath." Then come back to the breath. You can think all you want after you finish your practice session. During the practice session, thinking is not given free reign. During practice, you ally with the spaciousness that holds thought, the background from which thoughts arise and into which they dissolve.

When I was about seven, I spent a summer on my grandparents' farm in upstate New York. The farm cat had just had a litter and there were five tiny kittens mewling behind the tractor in the barn, terrified of humans. More than anything I wanted to hold one of those kittens and let it purr in my ear. So I went and sat. I sat for what seemed like hours and made no attempt to approach them. I sat quietly, with an open, friendly attitude. Patiently. I went back each day to the barn and finally, after a few days, one of them came out from behind the tractor, spied me, and turned right back around. The next day, ditto with another two peering around the corner of the tractor tire. The day after, the boldest of them very timidly, very slowly, ventured into my territory and finally after painstaking stillness on my part, allowed me to touch his nose.

Taming the mind is a bit like that. If you try to rush it, you'll scare it off. You need gentle, loving attention, patience, and a real desire to stick with the task, because more often than not, the going is slow.

With consistent practice, you will learn to observe more and more subtle details of your experience. It can be excruciatingly slow and tedious work at times. The mind is elusive. Tame it once, and it is easier to tame again, but it is never a done deal. There is always a discipline, a precision required to bring the mind back to rest. Even the tamest cat will scare easily when confronted by wild energy. Calm abiding requires a gentle touch, and dedication is essential.

Don't Meditate

That said, you can't really "learn" to meditate. Learning implies an effort by the thinking mind that will result in some new skill. Even in learning a physical activity like yoga asana, the brain is involved in placement, where to put this limb and how. Meditation is not a skill, but a state of mind that results from dropping skills: an utter spaciousness reflecting our brilliant original nature.

The discipline is in keeping mind and body to task with the patience to wait for the grace of surrender, to keep taking a fresh look at the reality of the present moment. "Trying to meditate" is an oxymoron.

When taking meditation posture, don't expect anything. Take the posture simply, with dignity and grace, but without hope or pride. You are not doing anything spectacular or particularly noteworthy. You are just sitting down, and for a period of time allowing yourself to become aware of your experience of the present. It can be quite boring. If it is, then just notice that. If you have an ecstatic experience of bliss and suddenly see the light, then just notice that, and come back to the present in all its mundane detail. The idea is that, in the absolute sense, one state of mind is not preferable to another. Whether you have thoughts of divine inspiration or of what you will eat for breakfast, the response is the same: notice what happened, and then come back to earth, the breath, and the body. The practice of meditation helps you to see the process of mind—seeing how the mind operates—as more important than its content.

Tilopa, one of Tibet's great saints and yogis, offers insight into this dilemma in his six points of mindfulness meditation:

> One should resist, or let go of the temptation, which at some
> point always arises in the experience of beginning
> meditators, to improve or make better one's meditation
> by meditating on tranquility, or on the experience
> of emptiness, or on clarity, or on bliss, or by
> fabricating or contriving any other strategy to
> improve one's meditation. All such attempts to
> improve one's meditation by "meditating" are cul-de-sac,
> and, as such, obstacles to meditation.

Keep the Practice Pure

Even though I find yoga and meditation practices to be complementary, I do not recommend combining the practices at first. Especially at the beginning, when you are learning a new practice, it is very important to stick to the traditional instructions. Later, when you have some experience, you can improvise a bit. But like any good musician, technique is required before you have the skill to play your heart out. Eventually, after some training, Shamatha meditation can be done at the end of the yoga practice, as the mind naturally rests after pranayama.

The shamatha approach is a completely different approach to practice. They are two different approaches to working with the mind. Yoga practice emphasizes steadying the breath—which will take you to awareness—and meditation practice emphasizes training awareness directly. Each one can inform the other. In the end, however, the goal is not to perfect the practice; the goal, if there is one, is to tune in to awareness. The practice is just a tool. You can spend your life crafting the perfect sword, but unless you put that sword to good use, it is not very helpful.

You may notice with practice that you start to develop a sense of kindness, acceptance, nonaggression, and peace as a result. Your experience will be different from mine. But these are some landmarks just to see if you are heading in the right direction. Too often, I see people who have a lot of practice under their belts, and who can't seem to get along with others. It makes me wonder why they continue to practice. If practice is serving only to turn you into an arrogant expert, then perhaps another approach is necessary.

Do I Need Yoga If I Already Have a Meditation Practice?

If you already have a meditation practice, you may wonder, "Why do I need an asana practice?"

Good question. You don't. You can settle the mind by simply sitting, but it is extremely difficult to stay present if your body is locked up. Many adept yogis in the Tibetan tradition have never in their lives practiced the variety of asanas that we in the West understand as yoga. Then again, many of them were born into strict discipline and were guided from a very young age to train the mind. Prostrations served to purify the channels, then sitting posture was the only asana undertaken. Of course this was in the context of many other observations and disciplines. The typical modern Western lifestyle lacks this context. So we may need a bit more help to attain the same level of calm abiding.

Ask yourself honestly, how often are you actually there for your meditation practice? You may sit there and feel calm. But how much detail do you actually notice? For most of us, sitting down to notice the breath is a nearly impossible feat. Trying to meditate without any background can be done, but for most Westerners, the process is so long that I find it much more helpful to start with a "moving meditation" such as Ashtanga Vinyasa Yoga. The breath combined with linking movements provides a resting place for a distracted mind. It is much harder to get distracted from the present when your muscles are screaming and you are trying to avoid falling down on the floor. Nothing like fear to keep you present.

The series of asanas in the primary series unlock the energies in the body that may have been blocked. As we grow up, we acquire certain habits and patterns, both mental and physical. We learn to favor certain experiences over others. We have weaknesses, for which we often compensate by creating screens to hide areas we would rather not deal with.

You could probably uncover all these areas by using sitting meditation as your only practice. But what I have found among Western practitioners of sitting meditation is that, more often than not, they are so caught up in the (often painful, usually distracting) experience of the body that their minds are unavailable. Or they are so caught up in their minds that the body is considered to be this "thing" separate from "me." Sometimes complete denial of the body is confused with being disciplined.

You have heard it before: the mind and body are linked. Even if the body is relatively comfortable, and there is not a great deal of pain, the slightest misalignment in the posture can create blockage on a subtle level, which inhibits the free flow of breath, and therefore prevents the mind from resting completely. Learning to breathe deeply not only helps focus the mind, but also relaxes the body. Ashtanga practice fairly forces the practitioner to learn to breathe deeply, settling the mind in preparation for meditation to dawn.

Understanding Ego

Putting the practice of Ashtanga yoga into context is an ongoing and very personal discovery. You may find yourself in your first yoga class for a variety reasons. Whatever initially attracts you will more than likely not be why you stay. Why you begin a self-practice depends on you.

One reason not to practice is to reinforce ego. And yet most of us have to pass through this phase. Ego is tricky. Pride and self-congratulations are its ambassadors. But some of us need a bit of morale boosting, and Ashtanga can be beneficial for this. It feels good to develop strength, discipline, and flexibility. Just don't get stuck here.

I used to get hassled by some of my fellow retreatants on Buddhist retreats. I would teach yoga asana to the meditation practitioners, and the group leaders would question me. They thought practicing yoga was too body-oriented, and so indulgent. These critics thought it reinforced ego, rather than taming it, as is the gist of the Buddhist teaching. Certainly this is possible. It is true that in creating a yoga asana, we strive for an ideal. But then dissolution occurs as we move on to the next asana, as long as we let it go! Ego development is not the fault of the system; it is in the intent of the practitioner. If the intent is pure, the results will be pure. Clearly my own approach needed some maturing before I could convince those Buddhist practitioners of the benefits of this practice. While it is sometimes painful to look back on mistakes, it takes maturity just to be able to acknowledge them. Humility is ego's antidote.

Ego loves to hold on to what it has learned. Ego says, "I know." Beginner's mind says, "Really? I never knew that!" Ego says, "Look at me!" Beginner's mind says nothing, just taking it all in. Ego is anything that takes you out of the direct experience of the present moment.

Benefits of Practice

It is said that the human body is a microcosm to the larger macrocosm of the universe. Each reflects the other perfectly and down to the smallest detail. By understanding your internal world in depth, you have access to the secrets of the universe. Becoming aware of your own particulars allows you the freedom to choose consciously to engage in behaviors and patterns, rather than being dragged along by a lifetime's worth of momentum. So by bringing the body back into alignment with the natural flow of breath, you harmonize the organism with the surrounding environment.

When you see someone who inexplicably inspires you, watch their mannerisms. I have had the good fortune several times to be an audience to His Holiness the Dalai Lama. Something about being in the presence of His Holiness is so overwhelmingly joyful, so inspiring, and so deeply calming. What is it that conveys this feeling?

The body reflects the mind. This does not mean that if you have a broken body you have a broken mind. It means that how you hold yourself, with all of your imperfections, reflects your attitude. It is in the manner of speaking, of using the eyes, an ease of awareness, efficiency of movement. Learning to hold yourself naturally with strength and grace will evoke those same qualities of mind.

You can't fake the internal world by creating the outer form; the idea is not to disguise. But you can mimic, and in that way slowly practice the external form so that the internal form will develop. Smiling when you don't feel like it can bring about the shift in mood that makes you want to smile. Making the body more flexible and strong will have a similar effect on the mind.

Through practice, you put yourself under the microscope. Whatever you see may frighten you. You have options here: you can run away and criticize the practice, in essence killing the messenger. Or you can muster your courage, face your demons, and try to learn something from them.

Practice as a Way of Life

As you practice and come to understand the profound nature of your own awareness, you may notice some changes in your life. Things that interested you before may cease to be a source of pleasure. Priorities may shift.

This is natural and part of the process of evolution, and yet, it can be painful. Relationships that once defined who you were dissolve or transform in such a way that they are no longer recognizable. Practice, if it is approached seriously, introduces you to your aloneness. Since the bulk of modern culture proposes everything under the sun to deny this fact of existence, continuing to practice is a defiant step against the standard view.

It depends on you how deep you want to go. As you become more and more sensitized to the subtleties of your environment, both inside and out, you will notice how certain influences help deepen awareness, and certain others lead to distraction. Experience is the best guide.

What I have discovered is that by relinquishing the goal, instead of paying attention to the quality of the moment, I often surpass the goal. I sometimes see students trying to force themselves into a posture: forcing the breath, forcing the limbs, focusing so much on the goal that the present moment becomes a fight. It looks so difficult! If you notice yourself getting caught in this trend, slow down, relax, and take everything a bit easier. Do not underestimate the power of awareness.

Have you ever tried to look at a star at night? You can't see it if you look directly. But if you shift your eye just slightly to the side, the star reveals itself brightly. Give up the goal, and strive just slightly to the side of it. Notice how the quality of your attention changes. The secret is that there is no goal. And even if you do attain it, you can't hold on to it.

Often I hear practitioners complain about not having time to keep a regular daily practice. Some even judge others for not practicing how they think they should, and pat themselves on the back for being disciplined and doing exactly as they were taught. I don't recall the part about there being a prize for the best practitioner. This is your life; your practice is a tool to take a better look at it. Don't worry about what other people are doing with theirs.

Practice is a support for life, not the other way around.

When I have no time for practice (which is rare these days), I sit for two minutes. I sit down on my cushion, and I wait. I wait for one deep, conscious breath. Time is unimportant. Quality of attention is imperative. One full, conscious, breath is more valuable than lifetimes of unconscious ritual.

I find that by allowing myself some leeway, I relax more. That's me. You may need more pushing. You may need less. The edges of our experience show us where we can grow. They are gifts reminding us to pay attention. This does not mean that we let our obstacles take control. Evolution is necessary. Your task is to find out where you are too tight and where you are too loose, and compensate accordingly. But unless you first accept them and allow them the stage for a moment, you won't have been properly introduced.

It's always easier to want someone else's problem, because from the outside, it may not necessarily look like one. But after the initial novelty wears off—it doesn't matter what the obstacle is—it's just obstacle, and we all have them. No matter what label it takes, however we conceptualize it, it provides the same experience: a structure from which we may view ourselves and go deeper. It's just a reference point, and a constantly shifting one. Essentially, a strong practice means a balanced practice. Our greatest strength is to be found in our most annoying weakness.

Sometimes we have obstacles that last a long time—years, decades, a lifetime. But with practice it is possible to see that within each obstacle lies the seed of our greatest gift.

FAQ

Why do we meditate with eyes open?

This is an awareness practice and so we are encouraging ourselves to stay present with whatever is going on. Eyes open reduces the chances of you zoning out. That said, if you find yourself overly zealous or distracted, you can lower the gaze until your eyes are open just a sliver. If you must close your eyes, just be aware that it's easier to lose track of the practice without that visual reference point. In this case I recommend using sound as the object of meditation.

I can't sit on the floor. Can I sit in a chair?

Yes. If you sit in a chair, find a relatively stable one (not too much cushion, which could displace your spinal alignment) place your feet flat on the floor, and try to sit without leaning on the back of the chair. Try to keep the spine upright and aligned, hands on the thighs.

I feel like all I do is think. I don't feel any peace at all.
What am I doing wrong?

This is normal. At first it may seem like the shamatha practice is anything but peaceful. What it means is that you are finally slowing down enough to observe your thoughts, so you are aware of things you may not have previously been aware of. It may feel overwhelming, like the rush of a waterfall. Simply stay with the practice of noticing each thought, and allowing that thought to dissolve as you let it go and return to the breath.

My legs fall asleep after a few minutes. What should I do?

It is fine to make adjustments to the posture in order to keep awareness fresh. Rather than making a knee-jerk reaction however, notice the impulse to move, and see if you can recognize that impulse as a thought. Let that thought go and return to the breath. If the pain persists, simply shift your leg position and continue meditating until the pain goes away. Then return to your original sitting posture.

Should I breathe through my nose?

You should just breathe naturally and observe the breath without trying to do anything particular to it. If it is deep, fine. If it is shallow, fine. Simply observe.

Is it okay to have shallow breathing?

This is fine. Simply observe whatever is happening. I like Thich Nhat Hanh's instruction on this:

> Breathing in, I am aware that I'm breathing in
> Breathing out, I am aware that I'm breathing out

Can I recite a mantra?

In many schools of Buddhism, practitioners repeat mantras such as om mani padma hum. But this is a different approach to practice than using the breath as the object of focus. If reciting a mantra helps you to stay more focused, by all means use one. But the practice of shamatha using the breath as the object of focus is a powerful practice because the breath is slightly more subtle. It allows more room for the mind to play, so you get more opportunity to observe the patterns of your mind. Think of the breath as your mantra.

I feel so tight or sleepy when I try to meditate first thing in the morning. What can I do?

It can be helpful to do some simple stretching or yoga postures, or breathing exercises before sitting first thing in the morning. Hip openers especially are useful for settling into a stable meditation posture.

How do I know if I am progressing in meditation practice?

As the great yogi Milarepa mentioned (above), signs of progress in meditation are a lessening of self-importance and a decrease in emotional reactivity. Other signs are an ability to stay present and focused, as well as the arising of a pervading sense of contentment or even joy!

I can meditate fine in a group but it's nearly impossible to meditate alone at home. Any suggestions?

Start small, and set goals. Like adopting any new habit, simply include it in your daily routine in small doses at first. Five minutes in the morning, and again in the evening. Once you start to see some results, it will get easier.

How long should I meditate?

This is relative to you and your life. It's better to meditate regularly for short periods than to sit for a big chunk of time once a month. Go for five or ten minutes a day, twice a day to begin with. Eventually an hour a day is considered a respectable discipline. But do what feels reasonable and don't set yourself up for failure with unattainable goals. Five minutes every day is better than an hour at the weekend.

I don't know anyone who meditates and there is no group near me. How can I keep my discipline at home?

There are many online resources these days. Check the section in this book called "Online Resources for Meditation Practice."

Yoga for Anxiety: Two Indispensable Yoga Postures

Anxiety has become a modern epidemic, and as a result many people come to meditation for relief. Meditation practice can greatly support an antianxiety protocol. However, if you find yourself too anxious to even sit and follow the breath, it's useful to have some tools to work with. These two simple yoga postures are my go-to remedies for settling down severe mental agitation and anxiousness.

Panic and anxiety are not purely mental events—they are physiological events, so they can't be treated with the thinking mind only. You need to learn to BREATHE deeply, and train yourself to come back to the breath on a regular basis. Mind and breath are intimately connected. If you can calm your breath, your mind will follow.

Through yoga practice you learn to settle the winds through breathing consciously. This allows you to relax deeply. It's pretty hard to stay anxious when you are relaxed. So while it is good to talk with a therapist about underlying issues, yoga can help with anxiety.

1. **Plan and schedule a time you can unplug daily.** It's so easy to get caught up in the communications technology that is available these days so that we never actually take a break from being "on." When you schedule time to get on your yoga mat, you give your mind—and eyes—a rest from the screen. This one reason is enough to see how yoga can help calm your mind.

2. **Create a calming and peaceful environment.** This may sound obvious, but a healing environment can contribute enormously to reducing anxiety. Find a space that is out of the flow of busyness, ideally with a view of nature. If you can't find a quiet place, put on headphones and some soothing music. Dim lights, especially if they are fluorescent. Sitting still or lying quietly in shavasana (corpse pose) can be a huge relief when you feel overwhelmed. *Shavasana* is a fancy term for: just lie down!

3. **Develop awareness of the breath.** Your breath is with you
    always, no matter what state you find yourself in. Make a habit
    of checking in with it. Notice your breath when you are on the
    computer, in the middle of a misunderstanding, or sitting in
    traffic. Get to know what it is that stresses you out, and then
    bring mindfulness—and conscious breathing—to that activity.

4. **Settle the mind and learn to disidentify with thoughts.** From
    a yogic perspective, anxiety is a disturbance of the "winds," the
    subtle energy channels in the body. Think of a jar filled with
    sediment when it is shaken: the sediment swirls around, clouding
    the water. A calm and grounded state of mind is characterized
    by clarity. The practice of sitting meditation is the most direct
    way to achieve this settled state of mind. When you ally with the
    spaciousness of the mind instead of the contents of the mind
    (thoughts), you automatically shift your perspective. But if you
    are too anxious to achieve this directly, it can help to enlist the
    help of the breath to help calm you down.

🍃 **Note:** Even if you already practice yoga or meditation,
    working with a therapist helps address issues from a practical
    perspective so that you can let them go. Practitioners often
    believe mindfulness will sort out their emotional issues, but
    in fact the opposite is sometimes the case. Deep practice
    may stir up old issues, and unless there is a container for
    these unruly emotions, it can be tempting to "let go" of old
    issues before they are resolved, which creates a muddy stew
    in the mind. Anxiety can be a sign there is something trying
    to come to the surface to be worked with.

Practice These Two Yoga Postures to Help with Anxiety

When the going gets rough, the tough take viparita karani—"legs up the wall."
This is my all-time favorite yoga posture, and my quick-fix remedy for just
about everything from jet lag to feeling overwhelmed, from exhaustion to
anxiety. It's the best way I know how to relax quickly and deeply.

Put your yoga mat up against a wall and lie down on your side in a sort
of fetal pose, with your bum facing the wall. Scoot your bum close to the
wall and swing your legs up. Essentially, you'll be sitting against the wall with
straight (or mostly straight) legs. Relax and rest for ten to twenty minutes. If
your legs fall asleep, cross your legs against the wall or bring your knees to
your chest. Come out by rolling to the side.

Follow it with child's pose: kneeling with feet together and wide knees, sit
back on the heels and place your forehead on the ground or on your folded
hands. Use cushions or folded blankets if you need support.

Online Resources for Meditation Practice

There are many resources available to help you develop meditation practice. Some are better than others. Here are a few of my favorites, which I still refer to on a regular basis:

Tergar Online teachings by Mingyur Rinpoche

https://learning.tergar.org

Pundarika online courses by Tsoknyi Rinpoche

https://tsoknyirinpoche.org/fully-being

Dharma Ocean online courses by students of Reggie Ray and Caroline Pfohl

https://www.dharmaocean.org/programs/online-courses

B. Alan Wallace free podcasts on meditation

https://media.sbinstitute.com

Anam Thubten free guided meditations

https://www.dharmata.org/teachings

Ocean online courses by students of Chögyam Trungpa Rinpoche

https://www.chronicleproject.com/teachings

DharmaSun online teachings by Choki Nyima Rinpoche

https://dharmasun.org

Recommended Reading

Classical Yoga Texts

¸ *Hatha Yoga Pradipika*
Yoga Sutras
Bhagavad Gita
Ramayana
Shiva Samhita
Yoga Makaranda

Yoga

¸ Georg Feuerstein
The Yoga Tradition
The Psychology of Yoga
Yoga Wisdom
The Deeper Dimension of Yoga

¸ B. K. S. Iyengar
The Tree of Yoga (coauthor Mary Taylor)
Light on Life
Light on Yoga

¸ Richard Freeman
The Mirror of Yoga
The Art of Vinyasa

¸ Kim Roberts
Ashtanga Yoga for Beginner's Mind

A Note about Classical Meditation Texts

Many, many classical texts on meditation have been translated from the Pali, Tibetan, or Sanksrit. However, I don't recommend trying to actually read them without the aid of a commentary. In order to find the right commentary, you must develop a connection to a lineage or a teacher. So while there are many classics available in English (and other languages), I recommend first establishing your community, then studying what the teacher is commenting on.

That said, there is one classic that I do recommend, for anyone. It's one of my favorite books of all time: Shantideva, *The Way of a Bodhisattva (Bodhicharyavatara)*. You also can refer to my guidebook, *Ashtanga Yoga for Beginner's Mind*, for developing an Ashtanga yoga practice.

Meditation

- Chögyam Trungpa Rinpoche
  Shambhala: The Sacred Path of the Warrior
  Cutting through Spiritual Materialism

- Shunryu Suzuki
  Zen Mind, Beginner's Mind

- Pema Chödrön
  Start Where You Are
  When Things Fall Apart
  The Places That Scare You
  Living Beautifully with Uncertainty and Change

- B. Alan Wallace
  The Four Immeasurables
  Stilling the Mind
  The Attention Revolution
  Minding Closely

Contemplative Psychology

- Bruce Tift
  Already Free

- Chögyam Trungpa
  The Sanity We Are Born With

Places for Meditation
Retreat around the World

~~~~~

Over the years I've participated in my fair share of meditation retreats. Here are some of the best meditation retreat centers that I've either experienced firsthand, or heard of through friends. I'll try to update this list regularly on my website, but please let me know if you have input! Feel free to contact me if you want more info.

Special thanks to John Morecock for helping get this list started! You can find him offering meditation instruction at New Life Foundation in Northern Thailand.

Americas

❧ Brazil

Khadro Ling, Tres Coroas, near Porto Alegre. A very authentic and traditional Tibetan monastery in the tradition of Chagdud Tulku. His autobiography is titled *Lord of the Dance*. Personal retreats are possible here. *www.en.chagdud.org*

❧ USA

Crestone Mountain Zen Center, Crestone, Colorado. Gorgeous zen center in the tradition of Shunryu Suzuki Roshi, tucked into the Sangre de Cristo mountains. Individual or group retreats offered here. *www.crestoneretreats.org*

Dorje Khyung Dzong, Gardner, Colorado. This is my all-time favorite meditation retreat center. Solitary retreat cabins in the gorgeous Colorado Rockies. All retreats are self-guided, however they will appoint you a meditation instructor for weekly (or more) guidance if you wish. *www.dkd.shambhala.org*

Insight Meditation Society, Barre, Massachusetts.
www.dharma.org

Karmê Chöling, Barnett, Vermont. Chögyam Trungpa
Rinpoche's original retreat center in the United States.
www.karmecholing.org

Karma Thegsum Tashi Gomang, Crestone, Colorado.
Three solitary meditation cabins in a breathtaking setting.
www.kttg.org/pages/retreat-cabins.php

Mindrolling Lotus Garden, Stanley, Virginia. Mindrolling
Jetsun Khandro Rinpoche is a very traditional and well-
respected Tibetan Buddhist teacher. Also see Mindrolling
Monastery, India. *www.khandrorinpoche.org*

Shambhala Mountain Center, Red Feather Lakes,
Colorado. Another one of Chögyam Trungpa Rinpoche's
original retreat centers, with a wide variety of offerings.
www.shambhalamountain.org

Spirit Rock, Woodacre, California. Founded by Jack
Kornfield. Down-to-earth vipassana teachings and much
more. *www.spiritrock.org*

Tara Mandala, Pagosa Springs, Colorado.
www.taramandala.org

Vajrapani Institute, Boulder Creek, California.
www.vajrapani.org

Vajra Vidya, Crestone, Colorado. Retreat center of
Thrangu Rinpoche, offering individual retreat rooms for
self-guided retreat, with guidance from resident lamas.
Also a traditional three-year retreat center.
www.vajravidya.com

❧ Canada

Gampo Abbey, Cape Breton, Nova Scotia. Founded by
Chögyam Trungpa Rinpoche, currently under the guidance
of Thrangu Rinpoche. Traditional three-year retreats and
other programs. *www.gampoabbey.org*

Sea to Sky Retreat Center, British Columbia. Self-guided
retreats under the guidance of Dzongsar Khyentse
Rinpoche's sangha. *http://northamerica.siddharthasintent.org/
sea-to-sky-retreat-centre*

Asia

❧ India

Bodhi Zendo, Tamil Nadu. A Zen training center in South
India's Perumal Hills, which also serves as the center for

Bodhi Sangha, an international community of followers of Zen-Master P. AMA Samy. Bodhi Zendo is open to all who practice Zen, or who wish to experience it. You can spend some days or weeks in silence and meditation, and experiencing the brotherhood of the Sangha. The founder of this center, AMA Samy, is both a Jesuit priest and authorized to teach Zen. *www.bodhizendo.org*

South Korea

Temple Stay program. It gives foreigners the opportunity to study in many temples in Korea. *https://eng.templestay.com*

Nepal

Kopan Monastery, Boudhanath, Kathmandu. Has famous month-long retreats in November of each year that have been the start for many people on the path of Tibetan Buddhism. It has other retreats as well. It is part of a worldwide Buddhist organization: Foundation for the Preservation of Mahayana or FPMT. *www.kopanmonastery.com*

Rigpe Dorje Institute. Kathmandu. The institute conducts two programs annually, open to international students. The two-month Rigpe Dorje Philosophy program is designed to guide students to gain a clear understanding of the Sutrayana and Mantrayana view. The ten-day Rigpe Dorje Meditation program is aimed at guiding students in the practice of meditation from the foundation of Shamatha through the progressive stages of Vipashyana, and finally the meditation on Mahamudra. *www.jamgonkongtrul.org/section.php?s1=3&s2=1*

White Monastery, Boudhanath, Kathmandu. Chogyi Nyima Rinpoche often gives free Saturday talks, from fall through spring, at his monastery, and has online programs as well. In November of each year he offers a ten-day seminar, often followed by a retreat at Nagi Gompa in the hills near Kathmandu. He is one of three brothers (Tsoknyi Rinpoche, Mingyur Rinpoche) whose father, Tulku Urgyen Rinpoche, was one of the most respected teachers and yogis of Tibetan Buddhism in the recent past. *www.shedrub.org*

International Buddhist Academy, Boudhanath, Kathmandu. This Sakya Tibetan Buddhist center in Kathmandu has seminars every summer, usually followed by a practice retreat. This is a very friendly monastery that trains monks to be translators and leaders for when they return to their home monasteries. *www.internationalbuddhistacademy.org*

❧ Taiwan

Dharma Drum Mountain, Keeling, Taiwan. There is a
Saturday meditation program once a month, and a few
seven-day retreats each year, in English. This monastery also
has study groups in the United States, Europe, and other
countries in Asia. Master Sheng Yen, the original abbot of
this monastery, wrote excellent Dharma books available in
English. *www.dharmadrum.org*

Fo Guang Shan near Kaoshung, Taiwan. This HUGE
monastery has occasional residential meditation programs in
English. They also have branches throughout the world, and
even a fully accredited university (University of the West) in
California. *www.fgs.org.tw/en*

❧ Thailand

Wat Suan Mokkh in Chaiya (near Surat Thani). Offers
traditional ten-day retreats focusing on anapanasati
(mindfulness of breathing) at a retreat center started
by Buddhadasa Bhikku, a well-known reformer in Thai
Buddhism. The retreat facilities are very basic, but the
center is in a peaceful and beautiful rural setting.
www.suanmokkh-idh.org

Dipabhavan Meditation Center, Koh Samui. This center,
associated with Suan Mokkh, offers three-day and seven-day
mediation courses by donation. *www.dipabhavan.weebly.com*

Wat Koh Tahm, Koh Phangan. Traditional seven-day
vipassana retreats led by an Australian Theravada Monk,
Anthony. Very simple accommodations at a wat in the
hills on Koh Phangan. *www.kowthamcenter.org*

Wat Umong, Chiang Mai. This tranquil forest monastery
just outside of Chiang Mai City welcomes foreigners.
www.watumong.org/web

Phra That Soi Duthep, "International Buddhist Meditation
Centre," Chiang Mai. Traditional three-week retreats and
ten-day retreats at this beautiful and famous Wat.
www.fivethousandyears.org

Wat Ram Poeng, "Northern Insight Meditation Center,"
Chiang Mai. Disciplined vipassana courses. Minimum stay
is ten days; basic course is twenty-six days. Taught by Thai
monks with translators. *www.watrampoeng.net/watrampoeng*

Wat Tam Doi Tohn, Chiang Mai. This monastery, located in
the hills thirty-four miles from the city of Chiang Mai, has
a traditional seven-day vipassana retreat each month. The
charge is by donation. *www.vimuttidhamma.org/en*

Tam Wua Forest Monastery, Mai Hong Son. This forest monastery, about twenty-two miles from Mai Hong Son, welcomes foreigners to join in their daily schedule. *www.wattamwua.com*

Wat Pah Nanachat, Ubon Rachathani. An international forest monastery started by Ajahn Chah for people who are interested in the monastic lifestyle. While it is not a meditation center, guests, both male and female, are welcome to visit and join in the schedule. *www.watpahnanachat.org*

New Life Foundation, Chiang Rai. A great place to stop and retreat when life gets you down. Also wonderful for those new to meditation who want a supportive community to get them started. Offers ongoing programs that include daily practice, life coaching, community activities, and more. Several times a year they offer scheduled, silent retreats from various traditions. *www.newlifethaifoundation.com/retreats*

Europe

☘ France
Plum Village is Thich Nhat Han's main center. His books and teachings are very practical and straightforward. *www.plumvillage.org*

☘ Germany
Buddhayana, Waidhofen. *www.buddhayana-ev.de*
Waldhaus *www.buddhismus-im-westen.de*

☘ Italy
Merigar, Namhkai Norbu offers retreats here at his center. There is also a link to many different Dzogchen centers throughout Western Europe. *www.dzogchen.it*
Lama Tzong Khapa Institute. Tuscany, Italy. Yearly two-month retreat guided by B. Alan Wallace. If you can't make it live to the retreat, you can follow along at your in-home retreat by listening to the podcasts that he uploads daily during the retreat. *www.iltk.org/en*

☘ Spain
Dag Shang Kagyu. Network of meditation centers in the Kagyu Tibetan tradition with locations all over Spain. *https://dskpanillo.org*

✋ United Kingdom

Gaia House, South Devon. Silent retreats, primarily in either the Theravada or Zen traditions, are offered. Many excellent visiting teachers. *www.gaiahouse.co.uk*

The Barn (Sharpham Trust Retreats), Ashprington, South Devon. This center has an ongoing schedule of meditation retreats, primarily with a secular presentation such as in the style of Jon Kabat-Zinn. *www.sharphamtrust.org*

Amaravati Buddhist Monastery in Hemel Hempstead, Hertfordshire, England. *www.amaravati.org*

Worldwide Retreats

✋ **BodhiCharya.** Ringu Tulku Rinpoche offers retreats around the world, including one in Crestone each fall. He is both a scholar and an accomplished meditator, and has written several books in English. *www.bodhicharya.org*

✋ **Pundarika** is the organization headed by Tosknyi Rinpoche, who travels worldwide giving teachings. He has an excellent website with many resources in addition to his excellent programs. *https://tsoknyirinpoche.org*

✋ **Tergar** is the organization headed by Mingyur Rinpoche, author of two highly respected and accessible books on Buddhism: *Joy of Living* and *Joyful Wisdom*. In *Joy of Living* he talks about overcoming panic attacks early in his life. He recently returned from nearly four years of wandering as an ascetic, and delivers top-notch teachings to those ready for a serious meditation practice. He offers retreats around the world. Highly recommended. *www.tergar.org*

✋ **Goenka Retreats.** Retreats led in the style of Goenka are offered all over the world at no charge (but a donation is requested). These vipassana retreats are based on mindfulness of body (body scanning) rather than mindfulness of breathing. *www.dhamma.org*

✋ **Ajahn Chah.** The website below lists monasteries that accept foreigners in the tradition of Ajahn Chah. *www.forestsangha.org/monasteries*

✋ **Dharmata.** The official website for Anam Thubten, a highly respected lama from the Tibetan tradition, teaching in English. Check the website for upcoming retreats. *https://www.dharmata.org*

Notes

1. Find more resources on my website *KimRoberts.co*.

2. For the sake of simplicity, I use the term *yoga* to include all of the yogic practices, including meditation.

3. *The Pocket Chögyam Trungpa*, Shambhala, page 4.

4. Rinpoche (pronounced rin-po-chay) literally *precious one* in Tibetan, is a term of endearment and respect used to address reincarnate Buddhist teachers. When appended to a teacher's name it denotes respect. It can also be used by itself to speak about the teacher in third person (Rinpoche said...). It is used essentially like we use the word *dear* in English. When capitalized and appended to a name, it denotes respect for the lama mentioned. It is used in a similar manner as when we might say, "Jonathan, Dear." When capitalized without a name in front of it, it refers with a sense of familiarity to the teacher being discussed (as in "Rinpoche said he would come this afternoon"), which can lead to endless confusion when there is more than one teacher being discussed. When *rinpoche* is not capitalized, it is a general term or used when referring to a teacher who is not specifically mentioned, for example, "There was a rinpoche teaching the program." The easiest way to think of it is like this: *Rinpoche*, or *a rinpoche*.

5. If you ever want to read a true adventure tale that reads like fiction, read his autobiography, *Born in Tibet*, where I got this story. It is the tragic account of Chögyam Trungpa Rinpoche's journey out of Tibet, when he fled the invading Chinese Communists.

6.   [See Part 4 Resources.]

7.   If you want a fascinating read about this era of Mysore and the development of both Ashtanga and Iyengar yoga, see *The Yoga Tradition of the Mysore Palace* by N. E. Sjoman.

8.   There is an exception to this view. In Vajrayana Buddhism, enlightenment is dependent upon allegiance to a teacher. More on this later...

9.   "Winds" refers to the Tibetan word *lung*. In Sanskrit this is referred to as "prana." Prana rides the breath, and breath mirrors mind. Breath and mind are two sides of the same coin— they work in tandem. So one way to settle the mind is to settle the breath. This is the way of yoga, working with prana. Sitting meditation takes a different approach by working directly with the mind, citta. So you can approach settling the mind from two different directions; or if you really want an effective means, use both.

10. Wikipedia.

11. A stupa is a reliquary that holds remains of great Buddhist teachers, and also a sacred architectural feature that is a physical representation of the mind of enlightenment.

12. Practitioners of Buddhist tantra, or Vajrayana Buddhism.

13. From *Cave in the Snow*, Ani Tenzin Palmo, page 130.